LILLIAN T
JENNIFI

2011

fortune & feng shui

SHeeP

Congratulations!

I want to thank and congratulate you for investing in yourself...and in the latest edition of Fortune and Feng Shui...your personalized horoscope book for 2011!

What will you be earning one year from today? How will you look and feel one year from today...and will you be happier?

In this little book Jennifer and I reveal many insights pertaining to your particular animal sign...what you can expect and how to protect and enhance all areas of your life for success in 2011.

And why stop here?

I'd like to also extend a personal invitation to you to join my Mandala...and receive my FREE online weekly newsletter...Lillian Too's Mandala Ezine.

You'll discover other powerful feng shui secrets from me that go hand-in-hand with the valuable information in this book. And it's absolutely FREE... delivered to your inbox weekly!

Lillian Too's Online Weekly Ezine... FREE!

You've taken the first step to success by purchasing this book. Now expand your horizons and learn more about authentic feng shui that really works...including more about the powerful 3rd dimension...your inner feng shui!
Just go to www.lilliantoomandalaezine.com and register today!

It's EASY! It's FREE! It's FRESH and it's delivered to you WEEKLY

Don't miss out! It's easy to register at www.lilliantoomanadalaezine.com and you'll also receive a special BONUS from me when you register today! I look forward to visiting with you online!

All the best!
Lillian

Fortune & Feng Shui 2011 SHEEP
by Lillian Too and Jennifer Too
© 2011 Konsep Lagenda Sdn Bhd

Text © 2011 Lillian Too and Jennifer Too
Photographs and illustrations © WOFS.com Sdn Bhd

The moral right of the authors to be identified as authors of this book
has been asserted.

Published by KONSEP LAGENDA SDN BHD (223 855)
Kuala Lumpur 59100 Malaysia

For more Konsep books, go to www.lillian-too.com or www.wofs.com
To report errors, please send a note to errors@konsepbooks.com
For general feedback, email feedback@konsepbooks.com

Notice of Rights
All rights reserved. No part of this publication may be reproduced,
stored in a retrieval system or transmitted in any form, or by any means,
electronic, mechanical, photocopying, recording, or otherwise, without
the prior written permission of the publisher. For information on getting
permission for reprints and excerpts, contact: permissions@konsep-
books.com

Notice of Liability
The information in this book is distributed on an "As Is" basis, without
warranty. While every precaution has been taken in the preparation of
the book, neither the author nor Konsep Lagenda shall have any liability
to any person or entity with respect to any loss or damage caused or
alleged to be caused directly or indirectly by the instructions contained
in this book.

ISBN 978-967-329-046-8
Published in Malaysia, August 2010

SHEEP BORN CHART

BIRTH YEAR	WESTERN CALENDAR DATES	AGE	KUA NUMBER MALES	KUA NUMBER FEMALES
Metal Sheep	17 Feb 1931 to 5 Feb 1932	80	6 West Group	9 East Group
Water Sheep	5 Feb 1943 to 24 Jan 1944	68	3 East Group	3 East Group
Wood Sheep	24 Jan 1955 to 11 Feb 1956	56	9 East Group	6 West Group
Fire Sheep	9 Feb 1967 to 29 Jan 1968	44	6 West Group	9 East Group
Earth Sheep	28 Jan 1979 to 15 Feb 1980	32	3 East Group	3 East Group
Metal Sheep	15 Feb 1991 to 3 Feb 1992	20	9 East Group	6 West Group
Water Sheep	1 Feb 2003 to 21 Jan 2004	8	6 West Group	9 East Group

CONTENTS

4. INTERACTING WITH OTHERS IN 2010

Sheep Focuses Attention
on Strengthening Family Ties

5. MONTHLY ANALYSES OF YOUR LUCK

Sheep Continuously Distracted
By Matters of the Heart

6. IMPORTANT FENG SHUI UPDATES FOR 2011

7. POWERFUL TALISMANS & AMULETS FOR 2011

RABBIT YEAR 2011
Clashing Elements
But Economically Better

The year of the Golden Rabbit 2011 will be a noisy year filled with the sounds of clashing elements. Global energy continues to be discordant. But it is a year when most of the animal signs enjoy the potential to make genuinely good advances economically. There is money to be made.

In fact, for those who are able to tap into their veins of good fortune, 2011 can turn out to be a bonanza year. It is a year that favors animal signs located in the secondary compass directions and is less favorable to those occupying cardinal directions. So two thirds of the animal signs can look forward to improving their financial situation.

We examine three important indicators to determine the year's outlook when the diplomatic, soft-hearted Rabbit rules, taking center stage and bringing a new set of energies to the fortunes of the world. After the dramatic earthquakes, landslides & volcanic eruptions of the Tiger Year, can we welcome in a quieter, safer and more stable year? Alas, if the charts are any indication, it seems not; there are deep rumblings under the earth; natural disasters and discordant chi continues to pose a threat to our safety; these calamities threaten different parts of the world. Earth's environment needs time to settle but for most individuals, happily the outlook does not look that dire. There is more good luck than bad for most of the animal signs.

Outlook for the 12 Animals

In 2011, those born in the year of the Sheep will benefit from the year, but only when there is an adequate supply of Earth element energy, so this sign needs strengthening with the **Earth Seal**. The Sheep enjoys the *Big Auspicious* star on its right, brought by the 24 mountains constellation. Unfortunately on its left is the star of *Yin House* which suggests some form of mishap. The key to overcoming this is to ensure that you are always surrounded by lots of yang chi - either music, sounds, socializing with others and avoiding yin places such as hospitals, lonely places and staying out too late at nights.

The Sheep also benefits from a good balancing of the elements, especially making certain there is Earth element near you. Wearing **crystals** (better yet would be diamonds) and being surrounded by Earth energy is excellent. Try also to display raw and natural quartz crystal geodes as these are especially good for you this year. In terms of amulet hangings, get the **Earth Seal amulet**. This will activate this wonderful 24 mountain star which has flown into your home location in 2011.

The Sheep is feeling very romantic in 2011. The feng shui winds bring the promise of a more loving year. Those already married could enjoy a second wind in their love life, while those who are single will succumb more easily to overtures. The more aggressive amongst you will also be on the lookout for romance this year. The peach blossom effect is strong, brought by the number 4 star.

Those born in the year of the **Boar** (Sheep's ally) have plenty to feel good about as the year brings great new opportunities for them to showcase their strengths and skills. There is excellent potential in everything they do this year because not only are there supremely powerful feng shui winds brought by number 8 helping, there are also auspicious 24 mountain stars supporting them. Boar thus provides good support for Sheep!

The **Dog** enjoys the same kind of luck energy as the Boar, as the number 8 also benefits this sign. The Chien trigram attributes are likewise energized and these two indications bring powerful positive developments for them.

In 2011 the cardinal East and West animal rulers, Rabbit and Rooster are afflicted by harmful energy and need to stay alert. These two must watch their backs, as both signs are affected. East and West are strongly afflicted directions.

The **Rabbit** (the Sheep's ally) in 2011 is hit by the nasty *wu wang* or five yellow. This is a negative star number that brings ill winds of misfortune and it must be subdued. The Rabbit must protect themselves against the wu wang star affliction, which is so strong it is reflected in the constellation of the 24 mountains. The remedy for the wu wang must be strong enough to overcome its power. It is unlikely that the Rabbit can be of much help to the Sheep in 2011.

The **Rooster** meanwhile sits on the *Disaster Energy Star* in the West and must contend with the Three Killings affliction. These are bad winds which must be subdued before Rooster can benefit from favorable feng shui brought by the number 9 star.

The **Snake** continues to have a good year in 2011 as it benefits from excellent feng shui winds. This is a year when continuous good fortune comes and brings continuous small successes. The Snake enjoys excellent indications of good fortune brought by the 24 mountain stars. Snake will definitely be on a big roller coaster ride in 2011.

The **Ox** enjoys a wonderful year as it benefits from the double *Big Auspicious* stars that flank its astrological location. This together with its number 1 star ensures that good fortune manifests strongly. Meanwhile, inviting a deity figure into the home brings good luck as the Ox has the *Golden Deity Star* in its chart this year.

The **Rat** and the **Horse** (Sheep's secret friend) also enjoy the promise of good fortune, but whether or not they can actually cause this good luck potential to materialize depends on their own inventiveness. But doing well in 2011 does not come without a share of the year's discordance. The Horse has a tendency to get sick, while the Rat's normally calm demeanor is put out of sorts by quarrelsome impulses brought by the hostility star.

The **Dragon** should sail through 2011 with a series of small successes. For the Dragon, heaven luck shines bright, so there could be unexpected windfalls. The way to go is for the Dragon to enhance for special luck to manifest. Wearing and displaying good luck charms will be beneficial.

The **Monkey** has a harder time staying ahead of the competition, especially those working professionally pursuing a career. Those doing business need to be careful not to get conned. This sign could fall victim to external politicking. The Monkey must be wary of false friends and ambitious colleagues. It is beneficial to carry amulets that fight against the evil eye!

Finally, the **Tiger** has to work at generating heaven luck energy by wearing the **Heaven Seal**. Doing so brings good fortune. This is a year when depending on their own instincts benefit them more than listening to others.

Carry the Heaven Seal Amulet to enhance heaven luck.

The Year's Four Pillars

The first indicator we look at to get an overall feel for the destiny outlook for the year is the year's Four Pillars chart. This offers a snapshot of the year and reveals the hidden forces that affect the fortunes of the year. To know what's in store, we analyze the eight elements that dominate the four pillars i.e. the heavenly stems and earthly branches that rule the chi energies of the year.

The preceding Tiger Year was a year of unstable earth disasters characterized by rogue waves in the seas and big earthquakes that began at the start of the year and continued unabated through the year... from Chile to Japan to Turkey to Indonesia to China and Taiwan. Last year, hidden Earth energies rumbled and brought tragedy to many parts of the globe.

In this coming year 2011 of the Golden Metallic Rabbit, its Four Pillars Chart looks rather foreboding. In fact, the chart is indicating not one pillar of directly clashing elements, but FOUR!

Yes, all four of the pillars have discordant crushing energies, with three pillars indicating Metal crushing Wood, instantly telling us that the Rabbit of 2011

PAHT CHEE CHART 2011 - GOLDEN RABBIT

	HOUR	DAY	MONTH	YEAR
HEAVENLY STEM	壬	庚	庚	辛
	YANG WATER	YANG METAL	YANG METAL	YIN METAL
EARTHLY BRANCH	丙午	甲寅	甲寅	乙卯
	FIRE HORSE	WOOD TIGER	WOOD TIGER	WOOD RABBIT

HIDDEN HEAVENLY STEMS OF THE YEAR

YANG FIRE YANG EARTH	YANG FIRE YANG EARTH YANG WOOD	YANG FIRE YANG EARTH YANG WOOD	YIN WOOD

The year is desperately short of EARTH ie Resource

is not going to be a docile one. The remaining pillar has **Water destroying Fire**. So in 2011, all four pillars that make up the Eight Characters chart of the year are showing direct clashes. This is a nasty indication and it is a clear warning for everyone to be careful and circumspect.

Travel and risk-taking are best kept to a minimum, and it is a good idea to be prepared at all times. It is not a year to tempt fate. This is a general but potent piece of advice for the year. Better to stay home than to travel. Better to stay safe than to take risks. Just glance quickly at the chart and instantly you will see that in the DAY, MONTH and YEAR pillars, Metal is destroying Wood! These are direct clashes and here we see both yin and yang pillars having the same clashing characteristics.

And then in the HOUR pillar, Water is destroying Fire! Each one of the four pillars indicates extremely negative outlooks for the year; so from year start to year end, and affecting all age groups, hostile energies dominate. This has to be a record of some kind; to have all four pillars showing a clash of elements with the heavenly stem elements destroying the earthly branches in every single pillar of the chart.

Disharmony is thus the prominent force of the coming year and despite the Rabbit, usually an icon of diplomacy, it appears that feng shui cosmic forces this year bring plenty of high octane anger and intolerance. In addition, the chart also show the presence of two Tigers, which suggests that the Tiger energies of 2010 have not entirely abated. We face a scenario not unlike that of the previous year, but maybe worse; clashing elements are always indicators of hard times, so the energy of the year looks discordant.

The chart shows Metal and Wood dominating, with Metal energy having the upper hand. The essence of the year is Metal, but it is neither weak nor strong Metal. Although we see three Metal, the Water and Fire of the HOUR pillar destroys and weakens the Metal. And because there is no Earth element present in the chart, Metal lacks the resources to stay strong.

There appears then to be a lack of resources during the year, and this of course is another bad sign. The absence of Earth also suggests an unbalanced chart, which is also an indication of turmoil.

With this obvious imbalance, the prevailing attitude during the year is one of unrelenting intolerance. There are three Metals indicating the presence of competitive pressures, but the strength of the Metals cannot be sustained because of the lack of Earth. This indicates that competitive pressures cannot be sustained and it is best to not be pushed into a corner by competitors. Try thinking outside the box instead of combating the competition!

The Good News

However, when we look at the hidden elements of the chart, the news for 2011 is not all bad. Underlying all the competing energy, lies the potential for the creation of much new wealth. There is hidden Earth bringing unexpected resources to fuel growth for the year, and there is also hidden Wood, indicating unexpected wealth.

Likewise, there is also hidden Fire, so the year does not lack for managerial capability. The exercise of authority and leadership plays a big role in transforming the cosmic forces in 2011. Results may not be evident in the year itself, but there is no denying the positive benefits of good leadership. As the NW patriarchal sector this year has the 8, the cosmic forces are aligned to help the patriarchs i.e. the leaders of the planet. So in the trinity of heaven, earth and man, *tien ti ren*, it will be Mankind energy that prevails and delivers success and results.

Herein lies the good news for those who are commercially minded and business motivated. 2011 is a year when plenty of prosperity-making opportunities are present. There are many direct as well as indirect wealth-making opportunities emerging.

Although what is apparently missing are direct resources as indicated by the element Earth, which is missing from the main chart, there are thankfully three hidden Earth element. This more than makes up for their absence in the main chart. In effect, the chart can now be said to be balanced with the presence of all five elements when the hidden elements are taken into account.

> What is in very small supply however is the element of **Water**, which was completely missing last year.

In 2011, Water represents creativity, intelligence and common sense. Because it is in such short supply, everyone once again continues to benefit from the **Water** element. This is what will create Wood which stands for wealth this year. Water also exhausts Metal which is destroying the Wood element.

Thus the source of wealth creation in 2011 is Water; i.e. creativity - original and strategic thinking which will open the way to mining the year's prosperity. Much of this creativity will come from the younger generation.

This will be a year when those who have just joined the workforce, and those who have recently graduated out of school and college will be the source of new ideas. And because it is the year of the Rabbit, when the East sector comes into prominence, it is likely that those born as the eldest sons of their families will be the ones whose stars will shine brightly. This year benefits the eldest sons of families.

Rabbit Years have always been years of appeasement, when conflicts arising in preceding Tiger Years get resolved. Unfortunately, 2011 continues to be a year of global political upheavals.

For the Sheep however, life is all about love and goodwill. This is because this sign is being infleunced by the romantic *peach blossom* star.

The Golden Rabbit Year is challenging and full of intrigues. Unlike the direct confrontations of the previous year, this is a year when unexpected betrayals and underhand tactics will be prevalent.

For the Sheep, it is likely that you will simply sail though the year oblivious to power plays and political intrigues. Those feeling this darker side of the year's energy need to have a positive and non-defeatist attitude; only then can the coming twelve months from February 4th 2011 to February 4th 2012 benefit you. Then in spite of discordant element indications, you can create and accumulate new assets.

There is wealth luck in 2011. The Sheep can harness wealth luck by making sure it is not short of resources and this is signified by the Earth element. What is needed is a keen eye for opportunities. Think outside the box to create new markets for your service and your products. The global business scenario is changing fast. New technology and applications of this fast-developing new technology is racing ahead at breakneck speed.

Globally, there is more than one prominent player in the technology game. Increasingly, the world is feeling the presence of China. Note that Period 7 benefitted the West, but it is the Northeast that is ruling the energies of the current Period 8. This Period favors China.

Both the year 2011 and the Period itself favors those who move fast and who have prepared themselves to penetrate uncharted territory, just like water. We borrow the term blue oceans to suggest the clever opening up of new areas for creating wealth. And it does not matter whether you live in the West or in the Northeast, if you can work with the cosmic forces of the year and the period, you are sure to benefit.

Water is Vital

This is once again a year when the element of Water will lead to prosperity, although not in the same way it did in the previous year. But those of you who installed water features last year and benefited from them will again harness good luck from the water. Note that in 2011, we are seeing three Metal destroying three Wood - i.e. clashing directly. The **Metal** of the year's heavenly stems continuing to destroy the Tiger's intrinsic **Wood**. On the surface this is not a good sign.

But Metal, when used with skill and under special circumstances, can transform Wood into something of greater value. So even as Metal destroys Wood, it can transform Wood into an object of value. What is great this year is that there is more than enough Wood to make up for whatever gets destroyed. Note from the Pillars chart there are 3 hidden Wood, so there is definitely wealth to be created and accumulated.

But clashing elements always suggest hostilities, so the wars of the world will not see any easing or closure.
In 2011, fighting continues with little hope for reconciliation; competition in the commercial environment and between companies and countries get worse.

Mankind energy can be harnessed very effectively to overcome the discordant energies of heaven and earth this year. All the resources required are available, the only snag being they are hidden and so, not immediately obvious. But they are there!

So here we can use the third dimension of feng shui - the powerful inner chi dimension - to transform and enhance the space and time chi of 2011 at individual personalized levels. Irrespective of the discordance of Heaven and Earth, those of us who know how can still arrange our lives to benefit from the hidden forces of the year. We can focus on the mankind chi within all of us - focus on strengthening it - and in so doing, more effectively harness the spiritual energy of the empowered self to overcome obstacles and emerge triumphant.

There are methods and rituals we can use to subdue negative energies caused by the four sets of clashing elements. We can also apply element therapy to bring about a much improved balance in the elements in our immediate environments; and there are symbolic cures, many made into amulets, that can subdue negative "*stars*".

The Commanding Star

A very positive aspect of the year 2011 is the appearance of the *Commanding Star,* an outstandingly auspicious star. Its appearance in the 2011 chart is brought about by the presence of the Earthly Branch of Horse in the Hour pillar and the Earthly branch of Tiger in the Day pillar. This excellent indication arises out of the ally relationship that exists between Horse and Tiger. Here, the Commanding Star suggests traits brought by these two fearless animal signs to the year. It brings good vibrations benefiting those who show courage and fortitude.

The Commanding Star suggests the presence of authority, power and influence luck for the year, benefiting those who find themselves in a leadership situation or those holding a position of authority.

Indeed, the year will benefit those who know how to use their positions of influence and power; so managers and leaders who have a clear idea what their strategy or focus are will benefit from this star, despite the clashing elements of the year. Leaders will find the energy of the year increases their charisma and their effectiveness. The exercise of authority will come easily. Those born under the Sheep sign will unfortunately be distracted this year. For them, the

Commanding Star does not bring much in terms of direct benefits!

What can be worrying about the Commanding Star is that both the elements of the Hour pillar - Water and Fire - are not good for the intrinsic element of the year. Here we see Fire destroying Metal, and Water exhausting Metal. Superficially then, it appears that the Commanding Star can turn ugly, bringing obstacles instead of opportunities.

Flying Stars of 2011

The feng shui chart of the year, which lays out the location of the year's flying stars in 2011 is dominated by the energy of 7, a weak star; but being the reigning number, its effect cannot be overlooked. The number 7 is a Metal number that represents the negative side of relationships, symbolizing duplicity and treachery. The number adds fuel to the discordant vibes of the clashing elements of the Four Pillars.

So while the Rabbit Year is usually a more subdued year, 2011 will see a tendency to confrontation, and violence is likely to continue. This is a year when intrigue and situational upheavals occur more frequently than usual; these are brought about by a higher occurrence of betrayals and unbridled ambitions.

It is a year when the center of buildings, houses and offices benefit from the presence of Water energy to subdue the strength of the 7.

Luckily, the number 7 is a weak star in the current Period of 8, so it is not difficult to subdue it. Anything of a dark blue color would be sufficient for keeping it under control. It is advisable to make the effort to suppress the number 7 in homes and offices. This will ensure protection for residents against falling victim to external politicking and trouble-making people.

In 2011 it is beneficial to activate the power of Water in the home. Invest in a small water feature to create a small presence of moving water in the center grid of the home. Or you can place a **Rhino** or **Elephant** there. Together, these three remedies are excellent for suppressing the negative influence of 7.

The luck of the different sectors of any structure is influenced by the new energy brought by the year's feng shui chart, as this reveals the year's lucky and unlucky sectors for buildings, houses and apartments.

The chart for 2011 indicates different numbers in each of the nine grids in this 3 x 3 sector chart. This looks like the original Lo Su square which plays such a big role in time dimension feng shui except that each year, the numbers placed in each grid change according to the center number. With 7 in the center, the other numbers are then placed around the grid sectors. This is what changes the pattern of energy in homes and offices from year to year.

FLYING STAR CHART 2011 - GOLDEN RABBIT

SE	SOUTH	SW
SMALL AUSPICIOUS	BIG AUSPICIOUS	EARTH SEAL
6	2	4
SMALL AUSPICIOUS	BIG AUSPICIOUS	ROBBERY STAR
TAI SUI		3 KILLINGS
5	7	9
5 YELLOW		3 KILLINGS
HEAVEN SEAL	BIG AUSPICIOUS	YEARLY CONFLICT
1	3	8
GOLDEN DEITY	BIG AUSPICIOUS	YI DUO STAR
NE	NORTH	NW

EAST (left margin)   WEST (right margin)

The numbers play a big part in determining the "*luck outlook*" of animal signs arising from the fact that each of the twelve signs occupies a designated compass location. Thus the Sheep person occupies the Southwest location which enjoys the 4 star number which focuses more on the emotional aspects of your aspirations. As for the 24 mountain stars the star affecting your year is the Earth Seal.

The stars of the 24 mountains are very influential. There are 108 different fortune stars but only a handful fly into the 24 directions in any year. These bring auspicious or harmful influences, but they vary in strength and type each year. The Sheep's Earth Seal, when activated, brings good feng shui and good resources for the year!

Houses and animal signs are affected in the same way by the 24 mountain stars. Some stars bring good luck, some bring misfortune. When your sign is negatively afflicted and your vitality gets weakened, you need to wear specific protective Taoist charms. These protect you from the affliction or they reduce its effects.

We have made different charms to match each animal sign's needs. What Sheep needs are strong Earth element decorative objects, powerful syllables and word affirmations that strengthen its good luck. There are other talismans to attract good fortune as well. These are highlighted later in this book.

Staying Updated Each Month

In many ways, the monthly updates are the highlight of this book; good timing plays an important part in actualizing good fortune and in avoiding misfortunes. To enjoy good luck during the year, you must update your feng shui. Hence, you need to know how cosmic energies affect your luck every month.

Every animal sign can be alerted to the high and low points of their year, and be warned against negative energy, as well as to spur you on during months when your chi energy is high. When to lie low and when to be go bravely forth are important to maximizing the opportunities of the year, so irrespective of whether the year is good or bad, you can avoid pitfalls and avoid missing out on opportunities that come your way.

The **Annual Protection Amulet** is to used to overcome the afflictions year and enhance good fortune luck for the year 2011.

Nothing beats being prepared against potential misfortune because this reduces their impact. Knowing the nature of misfortune - whether it is related to illness or accident, betrayal or plain bad luck - helps you cope when the misfortune does occur. What is better is that when you wear protective remedies, mantra amulets or talismans, these are very effective in warding off misfortune.

Thus an important aspect of reading these books is to take note of the spikes and dips in your monthly luck focusing on Career, Business, Family, Love and Study luck. The monthly readings analyze each month's Lo Shu numbers, element, trigram and paht chee luck pillars. These accurately identify your good and bad months; they generate valuable pointers on how to navigate safely and successfully through the year, effectively helping you get your timing right on important decisions and actions.

The recommendations in this book alert you to months when you are vulnerable to illness, accidents or dangers. We also highlight good luck months and this is when exciting new opportunities come to you. Knowing when will give you a competitive edge on timing. You will get better at coping with setbacks and overcoming obstacles that occur from month to month.

Improving Your Luck

Your luck can also be substantially improved through the placement of symbolic enhancers or remedies to the space you occupy. This is a book on the personalized approach for you to attract good luck. You will see as you delve deeper into it that there are many ways you can improve your personalized luck.

What is needed in each of the compass sectors of your home changes from year to year. In 2011, the Sheep should activate the Southwest with powerful symbols that activate the KUN matriarchal trigram; these would include images of matriarchs or powerful women icons; the double happiness symbol, the phoenix and other family-oriented images. This brings nurturing luck your way.

You can also place a big crystal geode in the Southwest to enhance the power of Earth; this should attract some superlative developments for you in ways that will make you very happy. The Earth Seal benefits you very strongly this year.

Your luck is affected by the year's flying stars (shown in the feng shui chart) as well as the elements of the four pillars and the luck stars of the 24 mountains.

How you react to the year's changing energies depend on the strength of your Spirit Essence and your Life Force. This year 2011 for all animal signs, both of these important indications stay the same as last year. There is no change to your life force and spiritual strength, so all those belonging to the Sheep sign will experience the same energy as last year in these two areas. Only the success potential for you has changed. This section of the book has thus been considerably shortened. In its place we are introducing a new aspect that affect your fortunes.

The extra dimension we address this year is to introduce you to your Sky Animal sign. In addition to one's year of birth animal sign, destiny and attitudes are also influenced by one's lunar mansion. This is represented by one of the 28 sky animals that correspond to the 28 days in a typical month. This is your Day Sign and it interacts with your Year Sign to add important new dimensions to your compatibility with others, and to your luck outlook each year.

Activate money luck this year with a **water feature** in the Southeast.

Your Lunar Mansion

This is based on the four great constellations that are the foundation of feng shui - the constellations of the *Green Dragon, Crimson Phoenix, Black Tortoise* and *White Tiger*.

The **Green Dragon** rules the Eastern skies, while the **Crimson Phoenix** rules the Southern skies. The **White Tiger** is Lord of the Western Skies and the **Black Tortoise** oversees the Northern skies. Collectively, they rule over the 28 Sky Animals, each having dominance over 7 of them. Depending on which of the 28 animals is your Day sign, you are under the influence of (and thus protected by) the Dragon, Tiger, the Phoenix or the Tortoise. These are termed the constellations of the Lunar Mansion.

Your Sky Animal brings additional insights to the kind of luck you enjoy in any given year depending on your profession or business. The year 2011 is ruled by the Eastern sign of the Rabbit; and with two Tigers in the Pillars chart, this is a year when the Green Dragon who rules the Eastern Skies is dominant.

Those whose Day Sign comes under the mighty Dragon are more likely to benefit from the Dragon. Thus bringing the image of the Dragon into your home would be excellent. The Dragon image was very beneficial last year and continues to be the celestial creature that brings good fortune to the year 2011. And since the Water element continues to be in short supply, it is as beneficial to have water and Dragon together, especially in the East of your home where it enhances the Rabbit Year, working with the Tiger presence in the Pillars chart to create the Zodiac trinity combination of Spring.

Determining your Lunar Mansion Day Animal requires access to specific calculations retrieved from the Chinese Almanac. In this book, these calculations

have been simplified, and any one can quite easily work out their Day Animal sign from the chapter on your lunar mansion. These offer additional insights into your luck outlook for the year.

Updating Your Feng Shui

Buildings are affected by new energy patterns each year, so knowing how to work with these new energies is what unlocks good fortune each year.

It is important to place remedial updates that safeguard your home and office. This aspect of feng shui is its time dimension, and because energy transforms at the start of the year, changing on the day of Spring popularly referred to as the *lap chun*, it is beneficial for all updates to be put in place before this date which falls on February 4th, 2011. This corresponds to the start of the solar year of the Chinese Hsia calendar.

Remedial cures are always necessary to subdue the effects of negative stars and malicious influences of bad luck numbers in the flying star chart. The location and strength of these negative influences change from year to year, so it is necessary to check them every year.

Three Dimensions in Feng Shui

Feng shui has three dimensions to its practice, a space, time and self-empowering dimension. These address the heaven, earth and mankind chi that make up the trinity of luck that collectively account for how luck works for or against us. If you want to benefit from total feng shui, you should use the collective power of all three dimensions.

Space dimension is governed by environmental feng shui methods - collectively practiced under the broad umbrella of what everyone terms feng shui. Here, it comprises the art of living in harmony with natural landforms and the art of placing auspicious objects with great symbolic meaning and element properties around us. Environmental feng shui takes note of compass directions on a personalized basis and use other methods that focus on lucky and unlucky sectors. Broadly speaking, it takes care of the Earth aspect in the trinity of luck.

Then there is *time dimension feng shui*, which requires our practice to take note of changing and transformational energies. These indicate that energy is never still; that it is constantly changing, and it is therefore necessary to always take cognizance of how energy transforms over various overlapping cycles of time; annually, monthly, daily, hourly and even in larger time frames that last 20 years, 60 years and even 180 years, which is the time it takes for a full nine period cycle of 20 years to complete.

Here in this book, we focus very much on the all-important annual cycles of change, but we also look at the monthly cycles; and we write this book on the basis that we are living through the larger cycle of the Period of 8. Broadly speaking, time feng shui takes care of the HEAVENLY cosmic forces that affect the overall trinity of luck.

Finally, there is the self or *spiritual dimension*, which broadly speaking depends on the energies generated by MANKIND. This focuses on the chi energy individually as well as collectively created or produced by people themselves. How we each individually, and together with others who live with us, empower the energy of self to either create good or bad energy.

In its highest form, the Self energy is believed to be the most powerful of all, and in the face even of extremely challenging **Heaven Luck** as is the case in 2011, the highly empowered self or highly focused person who has the ability to use the powerful forces of his/her mental concentration can indeed generate the all-powerful **Mankind** chi that can subdue afflictions brought by the intangible conflicting energy of the year's forces (**Heaven Luck**) as well as tangible bad energy caused by bad feng shui (**Earth Luck**).

The highly empowered self does not just happen. This too requires learning, practice and experience, and it involves developing a highly focused and concentrated mind that can generate powerful chi. This is **spiritual chi** that takes years to develop, but there are methods - both gross and subtle - that can be used to generate good mankind luck.

These methods are referred to as *inner feng shui*. Traditonal feng shui masters of the old school are great adepts at invoking the Taoist spiritual deities through meditative contemplations and meditations, reciting powerful prayers and mantras and using powerful purification rituals to remove obstacles.

Many turn to Buddhist deities who are believed to be very powerful in helping to awaken the inner forces within us. A great deal of feng shui history is thus tied up with Taoism and Buddhist practices in ancient China. However, this aspect of feng shui is usually kept secret by the Masters, many of whom are also expert at meditation and visualization techniques. It is their meditations that enable them to access their highly empowered inner chi which brings their practice of feng shui to a much higher level of accomplishment.

We found that many of the powerful ancient rituals for overcoming life obstacles, such as those using incense and aromas and the empowerment of symbolic and holy objects to enhance the spiritual feng shui of homes, found their way to Tibet during the Tang dynasty, where they were incorporated into their spiritual practices, especially those practices that invoked the powerful Protectors of the Land of Snows. These powerful rituals are now being revealed to the world by the high lamas of Tibetan Buddhism.

In 2011, it will be especially effective to practice this method of feng shui, as it will alleviate many of the discordant energies of the coming year.

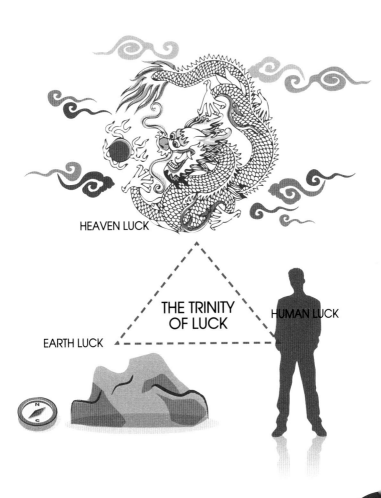

HEAVEN LUCK

THE TRINITY
OF LUCK

HUMAN LUCK

EARTH LUCK

Sheep Enters Nesting Period in 2011

- Water Sheep – 8 & 68 years
- Wood Sheep – 56 years
- Fire Sheep – 44 years
- Earth Sheep – 32 years
- Metal Sheep – 20 years

Outlook for the Sheep In 2011

The Sheep in 2011 will moderate its interest in the competitive world of work and business life with greater balance, turning its attention increasingly towards matters of the heart. Domestic issues and family wellbeing will engage your attention quite seriously this year with love, romance, marriage and domestic matters taking priority over work and business related issues. You will put work concerns in the back burner and you will be strongly motivated mainly by your family's well being. This is not a bad thing and in astrological terms is described as entering your nesting period.

So in 2011, personal fulfilment and joyousness comes from being able to satisfy the emotional side of you. Spouse and children will take precedence over office and colleagues, and you will find yourself preferring the staid and mundane chores of home life to the apparent excitement of corporate or social life.

It will be a transformation of sorts actually; one which is brought about by the feng shui of the year but which is also beneficial for you, because your horoscope indications this year point to a slowing down of business and work luck. Instead, feng shui winds are blowing love and nurturing priorities your way.

Your location is also visited by the *Peach Blossom* star which always suggests a rekindling of love interests, and a jazzing up of your love life! Some of you may be reading this in horror while more amongst you Sheep will feel secretly pleased!

No matter what your initial reaction, you will discover as the year progresses that you will become less and less excited by work concerns and more interested in pursuing matters of the heart. Health concerns brought by the interaction of your year of birth elements with that of the year could however adversely affect **20 year old Sheep**, although for **32 year old Earth Sheep** health could not be better. This Sheep goes through the year physically and mentally strong. But this is a transformational year for both as you will be motivated to try new things and to allow yourself to follow your heart. In other words, it will be what gives you real personal satisfaction that will drive you.

For the **56 year old Wood Sheep**, there could be some financial loss, but it will not be anything too serious. Financially, the year works out really well for the **68 year old Water Sheep** and the **44 year old Fire Sheep**. Both of you will experience noticeable improvements in your economic situation, and net worth could also increase. Both Water and Fire elements continue to bring good luck for the year.

For all Sheep, the year brings other rewards. You benefit from the star of the *Earth Seal* which visits your location on the compass wheel brought by the 24 mountains, which also brings you the luck of big auspicious on your right. This suggests that if you are married to, or are in partnership with someone of the Horse sign (who is also your secret friend), you can together capture this luck. What this means is that you can create something big together. On your left is the star of *Yin House*, which is advising you to avoid getting into any kind of relationship with someone born in the Monkey year. If you are contemplating marriage this year, it is a good indication as marriage brings you happiness luck and is beneficial. However, do consult the section on compatibility to investigate whether your intended will bring long term benefits.

The Sheep Personality in 2011

The Sheep's personality is influenced by the peach blossom star in 2011. To a large extent, this star number 4 will make you more reflective and introspective so you look inwards at what your heart is telling you. In spite of yourself, you become more emotional, and also less calculating. It will cause a transformation of your priorities so that in 2011, you begin to see the world around you with new focus. Marriage, love and romance will have a greater hold over you than matters relating to the ambitious pursuit of material success alone.

The driving force is the well-being your family or someone you love, rather than on making more money or on climbing up the career ladder. It does not mean you have lost interest in your work, only that your priorities are changing. Unlike last year, you are also feeling better about your love life and your feelings for the people who mean a lot to you. This indicates a lessening of personal tensions. You will feel less hemmed in by family and loved ones; instead you become aware of love energy flowing towards you and also emanating outwards from you. This is the effect of the peach blossom star combining with the *Earth Seal* star in the Southwest. Together, they create a flowering of matriarchal energy of nurturing and caring. The mother energy becomes very strong inside Sheep people, even those who are men, as they feel they should put greater store on what their heart is telling them, so emotional issues become paramount. This indicates a blossoming of new happiness vibes, what the Chinese describe as *hei*, a feeling of high caused by a celebration of some kind.

Your love life becomes very satisfactory and many of you will view your spouse in new light. Those who are married will inject new energy into their marriage and those who are single could marry or get into a serious relationship. The Sheep personality gets softened by the feng shui winds of the year. You will see those close to you in a happier light and even though your Life Force and Spirit Essence are weak, in some strange way, you will be feeling more comfortable this year. It is likely that the renewed sentiment of being loved and cherished will bring you new happiness.

OUTLOOK FOR
THE LADY SHEEP IN 2011

BIRTH YEAR	TYPE OF SHEEP LADY	LO SHU AT BIRTH	AGE	LUCK OUTLOOK IN 2011
1943	Water Sheep Lady	3	68	Happiness and money as well
1955	Wood Sheep Lady	9	56	Physically and mentally energized
1967	Fire Sheep Lady	6	44	Rediscovering the joys of life
1979	Earth Sheep Lady	3	32	Love and marriage brings new joys
1991	Metal Sheep Girl	9	20	A gap year to do your own thing

In 2011, the Sheep lady finds new meaning in her life as she rediscovers the joys of being loved as a wife and mother, and in turn giving love outwards as well. The source of her new happiness this year comes from rediscovering her family and loved ones as the peach blossom star brings love and loving energies into her life. The transformation taking this place is powerful and strong, and for many of you, it could even be life-changing. You will start to listen to your heart more, which eventually leads you to find profitable outlets for your creativity.

In 2011, those working or pursuing a professional career could find yourselves entertaining thoughts of giving up your job in favor of looking after the family. This reflects the powerful lure of the matriarchal energy, which is extremely strong in its effect on the Sheep person. To a large extent, this arises from the *Earth Seal* meeting the *Peach Blossom Star* in the Southwest. The three elements of this combination all point to a strengthening of the Kun trigram, which is the embodiment of the mother energy. But it is also because your horoscope indicates that work concerns are at a low level of priority this year. Usually when Success Luck shows a big dip, as it does for you this year, it indicates a loss of interest in that area of your life i.e. in pursuing success alone. In modern parlance, it suggests being influenced more by the heart than by the mind.

In any case, Sheep women are rarely overtly ambitious types; they may find themselves in a competitive situation, but they are not the sort to take up the challenge head on. The Sheep lady prefers to make competition irrelevant in her life by taking herself out of the picture. Those dealing with her should never make the mistake of thinking it is weakness that makes her refuse to compete head on. Sheep people, men or women, can be incredibly strong. Neither flattery nor criticism can steer them from what they want to do, but when it comes to their well-being, they are good at making choices. They are excellent at hiding their true feelings. Nevertheless, in 2011, the emotional aspect of their personality is dominant and in fact is the controlling factor influencing the decisions they make.

To them therefore, 2011 is not about luck, nor about how they succeed or fail so much as how fulfilled they feel about their lives; about what they are doing to improve the quality of their love life, their marriage, their family. It is these issues and concerns that come very much to the forefront for them. The good news is that the arising of these feelings reflect the effect of feng shui winds.

There is a great deal more happiness for the Sheep lady this year and it will not come from greater success or more money. This does not mean there will not be that as well - **68 year old Water** and **44 year old Fire Sheep** will find 2011 to be financially an excellent year. Other Sheep have the promise of Big Auspicious - something big coming to them if they should want to pursue that route. But 2011 is all about finding and keeping love!

OUTLOOK FOR THE GENTLEMAN SHEEP IN 2011

BIRTH YEAR	TYPE OF SHEEP MAN	LO SHU AT BIRTH	AGE	LUCK OUTLOOK IN 2011
1943	Water Sheep Man	3	68	Financially and emotionally great
1955	Wood Sheep Man	9	56	Tuning inwards bring new joys
1967	Fire Sheep Man	6	44	Good balance in your life this year
1979	Earth Sheep Man	3	32	Feeling very high & motivated
1991	Metal Sheep Boy	9	20	Taking time out to grow up

The Sheep gentleman in 2011 will be as smitten with romance as his lady counterpart, even if he will not want to make this obvious. The Sheep guy is equally influenced by the combination of the *Peach Blossom* and star of the *Earth Seal* coming together in the Sheep's Southwest location! In spite of himself, the Sheep gentleman will be ruled more by his heart this year. Reticent and shy he might continue to be, but the year will see him coming out of his shell, doing things he would probably not have thought much of doing previously.

For married Sheep, marriage and family represents a renewed source of pride and joy - and for older Sheep, the **68 year old Water Sheep** for instance, this comes with almost a windfall kind of financial luck too. For you, 2011 might well be a transformational year bringing not just a major enhancement of your net worth in money terms, but also the kind of happiness that might have been elusive in past years. Here we are referring to the possibility of a new love interest; or finding renewed happiness with your wife and children. However it manifests, matters of the heart bring a new lift to your existence.

It is the same, although perhaps on a lesser scale, for the **56 year old Wood Sheep** man and for the **44 year old Fire Sheep** gentleman - these Sheep will enjoy money luck. Sheep men in their mature years will discover themselves becoming more emotional in their responses. The power of the peach blossom simply will not be suppressed.

As a result, 2011 could see the Sheep gentleman being rather sheepish (forgive the pun) but also on a high. Love, or a new love interest is sure to create new magic for you. For the **32 year old Earth Sheep** man the peach blossom will have the effect of making you rethink your priorities, and for the **20 year old Metal**

Sheep, the year will be a ball for you as you take time out to grow up and see the world, with love playing a very big role in your investigations. In fact, it is extremely beneficial for all Sheep of this age group to take a gap year - take time out to discover yourself. Put off new responsibilities for a year to give yourself time to reflect on your options.

Changing Priorities in 2011

Success luck for those born under the Sheep drops drastically from OO last year to a single X in line with the Sheep's changed priorities in 2011. The *Earth Seal* star in your home location of Southwest combines with the incoming peach blossom star of 4 in the feng shui chart to make you think more about romance, love and family. So one of the more important aspects of the year's energies is to cause you to give higher priority to matters of the heart.

The Sheep who is engaged in professional or business pursuits is sure to feel the pull of other interests. The outlook on the work front does not hold as much of a lure as seeking emotional satisfaction. The pull of romance will be strong in 2011 and it will affect all of you. Some could start a love affair, and this might develop into something more serious.

Personal Horoscope Luck in 2011

The horoscope chart of elements for each sign is determined by the heavenly stem element of their year of birth. It shows how their ruling luck elements in their year of birth interact with the luck elements of the year 2011. This interaction reveals if five types of luck are good or bad each year. When the elements of each luck type interact badly with the equivalent elements of 2011, the luck is bad. When it interacts positively the luck is good.

In 2011, the Sheep's Life Force continues to be low, and it is important that this negative indication be overcome by wearing a spiritual amulet of some kind, perhaps a set of sacred syllables that carries multiple repetitions of powerful holy mantras. An excellent piece of jewellery to wear is the **Omani Padme Hum prayer wheel pendant,** which contains a million mantras in microfilm. This creates powerful protection that will ward off danger of any kind that might be life threatening. When the wearing of amulets is accompanied by some good deed such as performing animal liberation or donating to some charity, any danger coming to you will be successfully averted. Threats to the Life Force are usually karmic and they can be assuaged by a specific kind action on your part.

Unfortunately, the Sheep's Spirit Essence is also low, and this makes you vulnerable to the negative effect of wandering spirits. These local spirits exist in a parallel realm from humans, and while many of them are harmless, some can be harmful if you inadvertently anger them, through carelessly saying wrong things that get picked up by the winds, or perhaps by desecrating their homes by cutting down old trees or digging up anthills without proper ritually seeking permission to do so.

These worldly ghosts can only harm those with low Spirit Essence. The harm usually manifests as illness which cannot get cured or which keeps persisting, and you might also get weaker and weaker. The cure for this is to recite mantras or to perform powerful clearing rituals or pujas, and since you are unlikely to know how to do this, the best is to be protected against spirit harm. Wearing anything with mantras or sutras inscribed on them will protect you from the spirit harm arising from your vulnerability. Also should anyone out of jealousy use black magic against you, you might get hit because of your low Spirit Essence. Or it could safeguard you against love charms! Again if you wear a talismanic protection, you will be able to escape such harm. This is definitely a year for you to be extremely careful.

Your 3 other luck categories are summarised here. Note that Water and Fire Sheep enjoy excellent financial luck despite success luck being on the low side this year.

Water Sheep - 68 or 8 Years Old

TYPE OF LUCK	ELEMENT AT BIRTH AFFECTING THIS LUCK	ELEMENT IN 2011 AFFECTING THIS LUCK	LUCK RATING
LIFE FORCE	Earth	Wood	XX
HEALTH LUCK	Wood	Wood	X
FINANCE LUCK	Water	Metal	OOO
SUCCESS LUCK	Fire	Fire	X
SPIRIT ESSENCE	Fire	Water	XX

HEALTH LUCK - showing X indicates some health ailments afflicting you during the year.

FINANCE LUCK - showing OOO indicates excellent financial gains this year.

SUCCESS LUCK - showing X indicating a lack of success luck with progress coming to a standstill.

Wood Sheep - 56 Years Old

TYPE OF LUCK	ELEMENT AT BIRTH AFFECTING THIS LUCK	ELEMENT IN 2011 AFFECTING THIS LUCK	LUCK RATING
LIFE FORCE	Earth	Wood	XX
HEALTH LUCK	Metal	Wood	OO
FINANCE LUCK	Wood	Metal	XX
SUCCESS LUCK	Fire	Fire	X
SPIRIT ESSENCE	Fire	Water	XX

HEALTH LUCK - showing OO suggests good health with no ailments affecting you.

FINANCE LUCK - showing XX indicating some financial loss is possible.

SUCCESS LUCK - showing X indicating a lack of success luck with progress coming to a standstill.

Fire Sheep - 44 Years Old

TYPE OF LUCK	ELEMENT AT BIRTH AFFECTING THIS LUCK	ELEMENT IN 2011 AFFECTING THIS LUCK	LUCK RATING
LIFE FORCE	Earth	Wood	XX
HEALTH LUCK	Water	Wood	OX
FINANCE LUCK	Fire	Metal	OO
SUCCESS LUCK	Fire	Fire	X
SPIRIT ESSENCE	Fire	Water	XX

HEALTH LUCK - showing OX suggests that physically you should have no problems.

FINANCE LUCK - showing OO indicating that financially you will make progress and make gains in your net worth.

SUCCESS LUCK - showing X indicating a lack of success luck with progress coming to a standstill.

Earth Sheep - 32 Years Old

TYPE OF LUCK	ELEMENT AT BIRTH AFFECTING THIS LUCK	ELEMENT IN 2011 AFFECTING THIS LUCK	LUCK RATING
LIFE FORCE	Earth	Wood	XX
HEALTH LUCK	Fire	Wood	OOO
FINANCE LUCK	Earth	Metal	OX
SUCCESS LUCK	Fire	Fire	X
SPIRIT ESSENCE	Fire	Water	XX

HEALTH LUCK - showing OOO indicates you are in the pink of good health.

FINANCE LUCK - showing OX means financial luck is neither good nor bad - stays on course.

SUCCESS LUCK - showing X indicating a lack of success luck with progress coming to a standstill.

Metal Sheep - 20 Years Old

TYPE OF LUCK	ELEMENT AT BIRTH AFFECTING THIS LUCK	ELEMENT IN 2011 AFFECTING THIS LUCK	LUCK RATING
LIFE FORCE	Earth	Wood	XX
HEALTH LUCK	Earth	Wood	XX
FINANCE LUCK	Metal	Metal	X
SUCCESS LUCK	Fire	Fire	X
SPIRIT ESSENCE	Fire	Water	XX

HEALTH LUCK - showing XX suggests health-related ailments and maladies this year.

FINANCE LUCK - showing X indicates a small loss is possible this year.

SUCCESS LUCK - showing X indicating a lack of success luck with progress coming to a standstill.

Discover Your Lunar Mansion

How Your Sky Animal Affects Your Luck

Your Lunar Mansion is named one of 28 Sky Animals that pinpoints the Day of the Week that is favorable for you, and more importantly, it reveals what sky constellation you belong to, thereby opening up a mine of information as to the kind of people you work best with; the area of work that offers the best potential for success; and the nature of the assistance your Sky Animal brings you in any given year. Your Lunar Mansion is an integral part of you, so it deepens your understanding of what makes you tick, and how it modifies the attitude tendencies and outlook for your Zodiac sign.

There are four Sky Constellations under each of which are seven Sky animals, three of them primary and four, secondary. Those of you born in a Sheep year will work well with Sky Animals belonging to the Southern Skies and as a team or partnership, they attract good business luck.

At the same time, your own Sky Animal will likewise determine which of other Sky Animals work well with you. Basically, these are colleagues belonging to the same constellation as you.

Each constellation refers to one of four sections of the Skies, which are associated with the Four Celestial Guardians, the **Green Dragon**, who guards the Eastern skies, the **Crimson Phoenix** protects the Southern Skies, the **Black Tortoise** lord of the Northern Skies and the **White Tiger** who rules the Western Skies.

The Celestials and the Sky Animals mirror the Celestial Guardians of feng shui, and the Zodiac animal signs that make up the earthly branches of Astrology. This mirror effect strengthens specific types of good fortune. Sky Animals rarely bring obstacles as their effect is generally positive. They signify the influence of heaven.

Lucky Day

Everyone is born on a DAY that corresponds to one of these Sky Animals. In astrological terms, this is the lucky DAY for you. It is described as your corresponding Lunar Mansion and it reveals the influence of star constellations on your professional and business life from year to year.

One's Lunar Mansion is analyzed in conjunction with one's personal Four Pillars chart and the Four Pillars chart of the year. Such a detailed analysis is not within the scope of this book, but it is useful to know the trends brought by the influence of your Lunar Mansion (or Sky Animal) in terms of your relationships and your luck in 2011.

Compatibility

For instance, everyone belonging to the same constellation and coming under the same Celestial Guardian has an affinity with each other, and in times of trouble, one can depend on the other, sometimes even in spite of them being opposing signs based on year of birth.

Sky Animals also have natural affinity to their corresponding Zodiac animal signs e.g. a Sky Sheep has affinity with someone born in the year of the

Sheep and vice versa. The Sky Sheep also has affinity with someone born in the year of the Rabbit or Boar (Sheep's allies). This applies for all 12 animal Zodiac signs as each sign has a Sky counterpart!

Meanwhile, you can also be a secret friend of a Sky Animal. Thus the Sky Horse is the secret friend of the Sheep. This creates very powerful work luck as your heaven and earth chi blend well. This is a heaven and earth relationship. In itself, this is an indication of auspicious chi, so it is good for the Sheep to go into partnership with someone who is a Sky Horse.

Determining the Dominant Celestial Guardian

The coming year 2011 is a Rabbit Year with two Tigers and a Horse in its Pillars chart. This suggests that the Green Dragon who rules the Eastern Skies is dominant. This arises from it being a Rabbit Year and the Rabbit is one of the Sky signs belonging to the Dragon constellation.

The Dragon rules the Skies of the East and included in this constellation are also the Sky Tiger. The Zodiac Tiger whose location is part of the East also makes appearances in the year's paht chee. The strength and influence of the Dragon's constellation is thus very powerful in 2011. It is definitely beneficial to invite the image of the Dragon into the home in 2011.

Note especially that in 2011, the lunar year begins on the **3rd of February** which corresponds to the day before the lap chun, the day of Spring. This is an auspicious indication. This could bring miracles to the year and help in transforming conflict energy into something productive.

With the Dragon as the ruling celestial guardian, growth energy during the year will be strong. The Sky Dragon is the key to subduing all discordant energies brought by the clashing elements on earth. Lining up all seven animals of the Dragon's constellation is believed to bring greater strength for getting projects started and attracting the good fortune of the Sky Dragon constellation. This applies to the Rabbit, its seasonal ally, the Dragon, as well as to those born in the sign of the Tiger. Even just placing the three main Sky signs of this constellation - the Dragon, Tiger and Rabbit - would be extremely auspicious and it benefits to place them in the East part of your garden or along an East wall of your living room. Sky signs look exactly like their Zodiac counterparts.

Green Dragon Constellation

The seven Sky Animals that belong to the Dragon's constellation of the Eastern skies are the Sky Dragon, Sky Rabbit and Sky Tiger, as well as the Sky Salamander, Beaver, Fox and Leopard.

1. The Sky Salamander

This sky creature epitomizes the phenomenon of growth energy, associated mainly with agriculture and plantations. Any kind of profession associated with plants, gardens or plantations would be beneficial. This creature is a cousin of the Dragon but it can also complement the Sheep, so if this is your Lunar Mansion, your creative instincts will emerge. Your lucky day is Thursday.

2. The Sky Dragon

This powerful creature is said to be a magician, able to create wondrous things out of nothing more than dreams. Success comes early in life and you could peak earlier than you wish; the Sheep born with this sign finds strength in pursuing its own ideas and operating with high confidence. You can take some risks this year and there could be big things coming your way in 2011. Stay relaxed! Your lucky day is Friday.

3. The Sky Beaver

This is a creature that signifies stability and good foundation. If this is your sign, you should seek out mentors, people senior to you who could bring you "*follow my leader luck*". A Sheep born with this Sky Animal sign usually benefits significantly, because the Sky Beaver enhances your networking skills and these open pathways to many lucrative opportunities. Your lucky day is Saturday.

4. The Sky Rabbit

This is the most accommodating creature of this Constellation, usually associated with bringing family members together and establishing the bliss of domestic comforts. A Sheep with this sign will put family above work in 2011. Your lucky day is Sunday.

5. The Sky Fox

This crafty, alert and quick-witted creature tends to be at odds with the characteristics of the Sheep personality and there will be mental conflict as a result. Described as the heart and soul of the Dragon constellation, this creature can steer you to a high position and can thus be an asset. But the Sheep who is this Sky sign will be uncomfortable. Your lucky day is Monday.

6. The Sky Tiger

This is the creature is said to be born with a jade pendant on its forehead; so power and authority comes naturally to anyone who is a Sky Tiger. Success can be assured in the political arena and they also receive unexpected windfalls of luck all through their life, attracting help and support from family and friends. The Sheep with this sign might not be as comfortable. Your lucky day is Tuesday.

7. The Sky Leopard

This is the creature that benefits from being close to the Dragon; the wind beneath the sails, the faithful second in command. Sky leopards are almost always surrounded by many of the good things in life whether or not these belong to them. Nevertheless they are able to enjoy life's luxuries. The Sheep born as a Sky Leopard can achieve great success if they are discreet, loyal and keep their own counsel. Your lucky day is Wednesday.

Black Tortoise Constellation

For the Sheep born, if your Sky Animal comes under the Tortoise constellation, you personify the good life with little effort. This creates energies that make it easy for you to take the fullest advantage of your good fortune indications in 2011. It becomes a double bonus this year. The animals of the Tortoise Constellation are the Sky Ox (NE1), the Sky Rat (North), and the Sky Boar (NW3). There are also the Sky Unicorn, the Sky Bat, the Sky Swallow and the Sky Porcupine.

8. The Sky Unicorn

This creature combines the speed of the Horse with the courage of the Dragon. For the Sheep, if this is your Sky Animal, it indicates two extreme sides of you, for the Unicorn is at once your best friend and your own worst enemy. Sheep born people whose Sky counterpart is the Unicorn could have an exaggerated sense of do-goodness about them. You have to look beyond small grievances and take the big picture approach to attaining all your dreams. Make sure you do not lose out on the main chance. Your lucky day is Thursday.

9. The Sky Ox

This creature is associated with the legend of the weaving maiden and the Ox boy forced to live apart and able to meet only once a year. Sheep born people whose Sky Animal is the Ox will enjoy favorable luck in 2011, especially in real estate investments. The single Sheep could also find true love this year, but there may be small obstacles. Your lucky day is Friday.

10. The Sky Bat

This is a secondary sign of the Tortoise constellation but it is a symbol that signifies extreme good fortune. Benefits keep coming to you, especially if you are in the construction or engineering profession. Sheep with this Sky sign enjoy a life of comfort, living in a mansion through adult life. The Bat is greatly blessed if living in a temple or turns spiritual. There is good fortune awaiting you in 2011. Your lucky day is Saturday.

11. The Sky Rat

This sign signifies winter where yin energy rules. The Sheep whose Sky sign is the Sky Rat enjoys auspicious luck brought by 2011. A very auspicious year awaits you. You will be on the receiving end of some good fortune. Your lucky day is Sunday.

12. The Sky Swallow

This is the sign often associated with foolhardiness and danger as the swallow flies too fast and too high. This is the risk taker of the Tortoise constellation and Sheep born people having this Sky sign will be more impulsive than usual, and as a result, could rush into making ill-advised decisions. If this is your sign, it would be advantageous to reflect carefully before committing to anything new. Your lucky day is Monday.

13. The Sky Boar

This is a sign associated with the good life which gets better as you get older. Sheep born having this Sky sign are sure to be living in a mansion. You will enjoy good fortune in 2011 and the older you are, the better the luck coming your way. Good year to move into a bigger house. Your lucky day is Tuesday.

14. The Sky Porcupine

This is the policeman of this constellation, always conscious of security, alert to people with dishonest intentions. Sheep born people having this sign are artistic and hardworking, and very committed to what they do. This is a year when you can excel. Do not lose confidence in yourself in 2011, otherwise you might not have the courage to accept what comes your way. Your lucky day is Wednesday.

White Tiger Constellation

The White Tiger constellation tends to be vulnerable in 2011, hence those born into this grouping are advised to take things easy and lie low. The Mountain stars affecting the Western skies are potentially disastrous, bringing misfortune. Taking risks could be dangerous and the year itself already shows several warning signs, so it is best not to be too adventurous or foolhardy.

The Sheep whose Sky Animal falls under this constellation should be alert to warning signs; it is beneficial to take the conciliatory approach at all times. Also discretion is the better part of valor and it is better to be safe than sorry. This is not a good year for these Sky Animals to be too adventurous. Being a Sheep born, your year influence does not give you much protection this year.

The Tiger's constellation has the Sky Dog (NW1), the Sky Rooster (West) and the Sky Monkey (SW3). On a compass, you can see this reflects the Western skies sector. These are creatures of Autumn, when others are preparing to hibernate. In 2011, when the year is dangerous for this grouping of Sky Animals, it is a good time to stay less active.

The secondary Sky Animals of the Tiger Constellation - the Sky Wolf, Sky Pheasant, Sky Raven and Sky Ape - protect and support the main creatures with all seven coming under the care of the White Tiger. In astrological terms, the signs in the grouping of the Western Sky creatures are the most commercially-minded of all the Sky Animals. In 2011, protection is the keyword for those belonging to this constellation.

15. The Sky Wolf
This is an insecure creature with a tendency towards negativity, expecting the worse to happen. The Sky Wolf requires plenty of reassurance and it is this lack of confidence that is its worst drawback.

A Sheep who is a Sky Wolf must exert greater efforts to be upbeat especially in 2011. Confidence is the key to succeeding. Your lucky day is Thursday.

16. The Sky Dog

This is an excellent sky sign as it indicates a life of success. The Sky Dog always has a pile of treasures at its feet; commercial and business success comes easily and effortlessly and theirs is a life filled with celebration and merry making. The Sheep who is also a Sky Dog can find success in 2011, benefiting from the stars of Big Auspicious. But you have conflicting emotions and you need to be careful this year. Your lucky day is Friday.

17. The Sky Pheasant

This is another good Sky sign as the Pheasant indicates someone successful at creating and keeping their wealth. This is a Sky sign that is particularly suited to a career involving finance such as banking. This sign will also never be short of money as the Sky Pheasant attracts wealth continuously. The Sheep with this sign is sure to be rich but do be alert to anyone trying to con you of your money! Your lucky day is Saturday.

18. The Sky Rooster

This creature reflects its Zodiac counterpart, being naturally vigilant and watchful. The Sky Rooster is described as the eyes and ears of the skies ever alert to those who would disturb the natural order. You are an excellent one to have around in 2011 which is a year when your instincts are at their most alert. Sheep born with this Sky sign will be going through risky but potentially prosperous times. Your lucky day is Sunday.

19. The Sky Raven

This is the creature of the Sky that signifies extremely rich rewards from efforts expended. The Sky Raven is associated with success of the most outstanding kind. As long as you are determined enough, you will get what you work for. Sheep born with this sign need to work hard to enjoy a fruitful year in 2011. Your lucky day is Monday.

20. The Sky Monkey

This is a natural born leader who assumes leadership responsibilities without hesitation, naturally extending protective arms outwards. They are thus charismatic and attractive. A Sheep born with the sign of the Sky Monkey will be a role model of some kind. Others are inspired by you. Your lucky day is Tuesday.

21. The Sky Ape

This is the creature that signifies the important law of karma, ripening for them faster than for others. Thus the Sky Ape succeeds when they work and find life difficult when they slack off. Good deeds bring instant good rewards and likewise also vile deeds. A Sheep with this Sky sign will have good instincts in 2011. Your lucky day is Wednesday.

Crimson Phoenix Constellation

The Crimson Phoenix rules the Southern skies and its Sky Animals are the Sky Horse (South), Sky Sheep (SW1), and Sky Snake (SE3). As with the creatures of the other constellations, any family or business entity represented by this group of Sky Animals under the Phoenix benefit each other immensely.

Collectively they attract exciting opportunities; their best time comes during the summer months and working on weekends benefits them. The Sky Animals or Lunar Mansions of the Southern skies are:

22. The Sky Anteater

This is a creature that has the potential to exert great influence, but whether or not this can materialize depends on other factors. The Sky Anteater can be a catalyst, but it cannot initiate or spearhead a project or be a leader. But as someone supporting someone else, there is no better person. Sheep born with this Sky sign work well behind the scenes. Your lucky day is Thursday.

23. The Sky Sheep

This Sky sign indicates someone who will eventually become deeply spiritual or psychic. When developed to its fullest potential, such a person becomes incredibly charismatic - easily becoming an iconic source of inspiration to others. A Sheep born with this Sky sign has the potential to achieve brilliance as industry leaders or politicians. Your lucky day is Friday.

24. The Sky Roebuck

This is a creature of healing, someone who has the gift to mend broken hearts and emotionally distraught people. Those with this Sky sign have calm dispositions so a Sheep born under this Sky sign will be an excellent calming influence on anyone. This sign usually do extremely well as counselors. Your lucky day is Saturday.

25. The Sky Horse

This is a lovely Sky sign loved by many people. Also referred to as the mediator of the skies, the Sky Horse takes everyone for a joyride, helping others forget their grievances with great effectiveness. A Sheep born with this sign tends to be more adventurous than usual. Your lucky day is Sunday.

26. The Sky Deer

This is a generous creature whose spirit of giving endears it to many others. The Sky Deer is often also associated with those who make it to a high position and then using their influence and success to benefit many others. A Sheep born who has this Sky sign is sure to have this dimension of generosity in their personality. Your lucky day is Monday.

27. The Sky Snake

This creature represents imperial authority. The Sky Snake travels on the wings of the Phoenix, always ready to receive the applause and adoration of others. Sky Snakes enjoy the destiny of personal advancement, especially in the political arena. A Sheep who is a Sky Snake should benefit in 2011. Your lucky day is Tuesday.

28. The Sky Worm

Humble as this creature may sound, the Sky Worm aims high, and when it succeeds, it does so with panache and great style. This is the great surprise of the constellation of Lunar Mansions because those born under this sign have great perseverance and amazing courage to take risks; success for them comes with a vengeance! The Sheep with this sign should do well in 2011. Your lucky day is Wednesday.

Determining Your Sky Animal Sign

Example: If your day of birth is
18th June 1979

1. Get the corresponding number for your
    month and **year** from **Table 1**. Thus the
    number for **June** is **10**, and the number for
    the year **1979** is **19**.

2. Next, add the numbers of the month and
    the year to the day, which is **18**. Thus **10 +
    19 + 18 = 47**.

3. Next determine if your year of birth 1979 is
    a leap year; if it is, and you were born after
    March 1st, add 1. Here 1979 is not a leap
    year, and you were born after **March 1st**, so
    here you do not add 1 to **47**.

4. As **47** is lower than **56** but higher than
    28, you need to subtract 28 from 47. Thus
    47 - 28 = 19. So note that for you, the Sky
    Animal is number **19**.

To explain this part of the calculation note that since there are 28 animals, any number higher than 28 should deduct 28 and any number higher than 56 which is 28 x 2, should deduct 56 from the total to reach a number that is lower than 28. **This will indicate your Lunar Mansion number.**

Once you have your number, which in this example is 19, your Sky Animal (or Lunar Mansion) is the one corresponding to the number in Table 2.

In this example of someone born on 18th June 1979, your Sky Animal is the **Sky Raven** and you belong to the Constellation of the **White Tiger** of the Western skies. Your lucky day is **Monday** and you belong to the constellation season of **Autumn**.

Meanwhile, based on your year of birth, you are born under the Zodiac sign of the **Earth Sheep**.

TABLE 1
To Determine the Animal of Your Day of Birth

MONTH	YEAR	YEAR	YEAR	YEAR	YEAR	NO.
-	1920*	1942	-	1987	2009	1
FEB, MAR	-	1943	1965	1988*	2010	2
-	1921	1944*	1966	-	2011	3
-	1922	-	1967	1989	2012*	4
APRIL	1923	1945	1968*	1990		5
-	1924*	1946	-	1991	2013	6
MAY	-	1947	1969	1992*	2014	7
-	1925	1948*	1970	-	2015	8
-	1926	-	1971	1993	2016*	9
JUNE	1927	1949	1972*	1994		10
-	1928*	1950		1995	2017	11
JULY	-	1951	1973	1996*	2018	12
-	1929	1952*	1974	-	2019	13
-	1930	-	1975	1997	2020*	14
AUGUST	1931	1953	1976*	1998		15
-	1932*	1954		1999	2021	16
-	-	1955	1977	2000*	2022	17
SEPTEMBER	1933	1956*	1978		2023	18
-	1934	-	1979	2001	2024*	19
OCTOBER	1935	1957	1980*	2002		20
-	1936*	1958		2003	2025	21
-	-	1959	1981	2004*	2026	22
NOVEMBER	1937	1960*	1982	-	2027	23
-	1938	-	1983	2005	2028*	24
DECEMBER	1939	1961	1984*	2006	-	25
-	1940*	1962		2007	2029	26
JANUARY	-	1963	1985	2008*	2030	27
-	1941	1964*	1986	-	2031	28

* indicates a leap year

TABLE 2
The 28 Animals of the Four Constellations

**FAMILY OF THE GREEN DRAGON
RULING THE SEASON OF SPRING**

Lunar Mansion Constellations
of the **Eastern** skies

1.   **Sky Salamander** THURSDAY
2.   **Sky Dragon** FRIDAY
3.   **Sky Beaver** SATURDAY
4.   **Sky Rabbit** SUNDAY
5.   **Sky Fox** MONDAY
6.   **Sky Tiger** TUESDAY
7.   **Sky Leopard** WEDNESDAY

**FAMILY OF THE BLACK TORTOISE
RULING THE SEASON OF WINTER**

Lunar Mansion Constellations
of the **Northern** skies

8.   **Sky Unicorn** THURSDAY
9.   **Sky Ox** FRIDAY
10. **Sky Bat** SATURDAY
11. **Sky Rat** SUNDAY
12. **Sky Swallow** MONDAY
13. **Sky Boar** TUESDAY
14. **Sky Porcupine** WEDNESDAY

**FAMILY OF THE WHITE TIGER
RULING THE SEASON OF AUTUMN**

Lunar Mansion Constellations
of the **Western** skies

15. **Sky Wolf** THURSDAY
16. **Sky Dog** FRIDAY
17. **Sky Pheasant** SATURDAY
18. **Sky Rooster** SUNDAY
19. **Sky Raven** MONDAY
20. **Sky Monkey** TUESDAY
21. **Sky Ape** WEDNESDAY

**FAMILY OF THE CRIMSON PHOENIX
RULING THE SEASON OF SUMMER**

Lunar Mansion Constellations
of the **Southern** skies

22. **Sky Ant Eater** THURSDAY
23. **Sky Sheep** FRIDAY
24. **Sky Antler** SATURDAY
25. **Sky Horse** SUNDAY
26. **Sky Deer** MONDAY
27. **Sky Snake** TUESDAY
28. **Sky Worm** WEDNESDAY

Interacting With Others In 2011

Sheep Focuses Attention On Strengthening Family Ties

Many factors affect how one animal sign gets along with another and the Chinese believe that much of this has to do with astrological forces and influences of a particular year. The varying factors result in a difference in compatibility levels each year and while it is impossible to take note of everything, the key variables to note are one's chi energy essence and whether the year's constellations are making you feel positive and good about yourself. The influence of the YEAR on the compatibilities of relationships is thus important; you cannot ignore the annual chi effect on the way you interact with your loved ones and family.

New energies influence the way you treat people, in turn determining how they respond to you. How you interact with close friends and loved ones is affected by your mental and physical state. So how you get on with your partner, your spouse, parents, children, siblings, relatives and friends are affected by your fortunes in any given year. But relationships are important because how these work out create important inputs to your happiness.

Understanding compatibility make you more understanding; when differences crop up, these need not be taken to heart. Good vibes make you tolerant while afflictive energies and negative stars suffered by others can make them seem tiresome.

Annual energy also influences what kind of people you will have greater or lesser affinity with. In some years you might feel an inexplicable aversion to someone you may always have liked and loved; or be attracted to someone you have always found annoying! Usually of course, the affinity groupings, secret friends alliances and ideal soul mate pairings of the Zodiac exert strong influences too, but annual chi plays a dominant role in swaying your thinking and those of others. They can make you more argumentative or make you more loving.

People tend to be more or less tolerant or selfish, cold or warm depending on the way things turn out for them from year to year. When life and work goes well, we become better disposed towards others. Then, even a natural zodiac enemy can become a soulmate, if only for a short period of time. Likewise, when one is being challenged by big problems, even the slightest provocation can lead to anger. Zodiac friends and allies might even then appear to be insufferable. A falling out between horoscope allies is thus not impossible.

In this section we examine the Sheep's personal relationships with the other eleven signs in 2011. This is a year when Sheep's focus is very much on enhancing family relationships.

Zodiac Influences
1. Alliance of Allies
2. Zodiac Soulmates
3. Secret Friends
4. Astrology Enemies
5. Peach Blossom
6. Seasonal Trinity

1. Alliance of Allies

Four affinity groupings of animal signs form an Alliance of natural allies in the Horoscope. The three signs possess similar thought processes and aspirations and share similar goals. They support each other and can be depended on.

When all three signs enjoy good fortune in any year, it makes the alliance strong, and if there is an alliance within a family unit, such as amongst siblings, or with the spouses and their child, the family is extremely supportive, giving strength to each other. In good years, auspicious luck gets multiplied. Allies always get along. Any falling out is temporary. They trust each other and close ranks against external threats. Good astrological feng shui comes from carrying the image of your allies, especially when they are going through good years.

ALLY GROUPINGS	ANIMALS	CHARACTERISTICS
COMPETITORS	Rat, Dragon, Monkey	Competent, Tough, Resolute
INTELLECTUALS	Ox, Snake, Rooster	Generous, Focused, Resilient
ENTHUSIASTS	Dog, Tiger, Horse	Aggressive, Rebellious, Coy
DIPLOMATS	Boar, Sheep, Rabbit	Creative, Kind, Emotional

The Sheep and its allies together make up the numbers 4, 8 and 5 which indicate that in 2011, it is the Boar who has the strongest and luckiest star indication. The Sheep enjoys the luck of romance in 2011 but the Rabbit is afflicted by the *wu wang*. The Sheep and Boar each enjoy the auspicious stars of the 24 mountains. So the strongest link in this alliance is the Boar, who has the power of the number 8 star, but Sheep is also good. In 2011, this is not a strong alliance. The Boar must carry the year.

The alliance of allies as a group can weather the storms of this challenging year more successfully. When all members of the alliance within your circle of friends team up, their collective good energy gets magnified. When your work associates and you comprise this grouping of Sheep, Rabbit and Boar, the year becomes more amiable. If there are three of you in a family, or within the same department of a company, the alliance

Rabbit, Sheep and Boar are Allies of the Chinese Zodiac.

can be activated to benefit every member. In this alliance, the Rabbit will naturally lean on the others in 2011, but the Sheep and the Boar provide enough strength for all.

2. Zodiac Soulmates

Six pairs of animal signs create six Zodiac Houses of yin and yang soul mates. Each pair creates powerful bonding at a cosmic level. Marriages or business unions between people belonging to the same Zodiac House are extremely auspicious. In a marriage, there is promise of great happiness. In a commercial partnership, it promises wealth and success. This pairing is good between professional colleagues and siblings.

The strength of each pair is different; with their own defining strength, and with some making better commercial than marriage partners. How successful you are as a pair depends on how you bond. The table on the following page summarizes the key strength of each Zodiac house.

A coming together of yin Sheep with its soul mate the yang Horse creates the House of Passion & Sexuality. It is an exciting alliance and together these two animal signs create a romantic life together. As their House name suggests, this is a passionate pair for whom

HOUSES OF PAIRED SOULMATES

ANIMALS	YIN/ YANG	ZODIAC HOUSE OF CREATIVITY	TARGET UNLEASHED
Rat	YANG	HOUSE OF CREATIVITY & CLEVERNESS	The Rat initiates
Ox	YIN		The Ox completes
Tiger	YANG	HOUSE OF GROWTH & DEVELOPMENT	The Tiger employs force
Rabbit	YIN		The Rabbit uses diplomacy
Dragon	YANG	HOUSE OF MAGIC & SPRITITUALITY	The Dragon creates magic
Snake	YIN		The Snake creates mystery
Horse	YANG	HOUSE OF PASSION & SEXUALITY	The Horse embodies male energy
Sheep	YIN		The Sheep is the female energy
Monkey	YANG	HOUSE OF CAREER & COMMERCE	The Monkey creates strategy
Rooster	YIN		The Rooster get things moving
Dog	YANG	HOUSE OF DOMESTICITY	The Dog works to provide
Boar	YIN		The Boar enjoys what is created

2011 brings good times. These two have a special bond and in 2011 the Horse has enough inner strength to sustain them both. The Sheep focuses its energies on the family and works at strengthening bonds with spouse and children.

3. Secret Friends

There are six sets of a *secret friendship* that exists between the animal signs of the Zodiac. Between them a very powerful affinity exists making them excellent for each other. Love, respect and goodwill flow freely between secret friends; and they create wonderful happiness vibes for each other in a marriage. Once forged, it is a bond that is hard to break; and even when they themselves want to break, it will be hard for either party to fully walk away. This pair of signs will stick together through thick and thin.

PAIRINGS OF SECRET FRIENDS

🐀	Rat	Ox	🐂
🐖	Boar	Tiger	🐅
🐕	Dog	Rabbit	🐇
🐉	Dragon	Rooster	🐓
🐍	Snake	Monkey	🐒
🐎	**Horse**	**Sheep**	🐐

In the pairing of secret friends, the Sheep is again paired with the Horse. It is obvious there is a strong cosmic bond between these two animal signs and in 2011, they have a great romp. The Horse is fiercely passionate as a partner, so the Sheep is likely to enjoy a great deal of loving from the Horse. This suits the Sheep fine as 2011 is when the romantic star brings great passion in all aspects of their lives. It is indeed a very happy time.

4. Astrological Enemies

Then there are the astrological enemies of the Horoscope. This is the sign that directly confronts yours in the Astrology Compass. For the Sheep your enemy is the Ox. Note that the enemy does not necessarily harm you; it only means someone

PAIRINGS OF ASTROLOGICAL ENEMIES

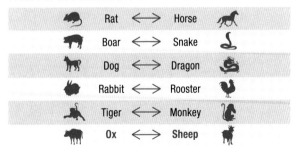

Rat	⟷	Horse
Boar	⟷	Snake
Dog	⟷	Dragon
Rabbit	⟷	Rooster
Tiger	⟷	Monkey
Ox	⟷	Sheep

of this sign can never be of any real help to you. But note that the enmity between the Sheep and the Ox is not as severe as others as they are both of the Earth element. There is a six year gap between the natural foes of the Zodiac. A marriage between them is usually not recommended. They rarely have sincere intentions towards one another. Marriage between the Sheep with an Ox is unlikely to bring lasting happiness unless other indications in their respective Paht Chee charts suggest otherwise. Pairings between arrows of antagonism are usually discouraged by those who investigate Zodiac compatibilities. The Sheep is advised to refrain from getting involved with an Ox person.

As a business partnership, the pairing is likely to be problematic, and in the event of a split, the separation can be acrimonious even if they start out as best friends. In 2011 however, the Ox and the Sheep will find themselves enjoying a rather amicable relationship.

5. Peach Blossom Links

Each of the Alliance of Allies has a special relationship with one of the four primary signs of Horse, Rat, Rooster and Rabbit in that these are the symbolic representations of love and romance for one Alliance group of animal signs. In the Horoscope, they are referred to as peach blossom animals and the presence of their images in the homes of the matching Alliance of Allies brings peach blossom luck which is associated with love and romance.

The Sheep belongs to the Alliance of Rabbit, Boar and Sheep, which has the Rat as their peach blossom link. The Sheep will benefit from associating with anyone born in the Rat year, and will also benefit from placing a painting or image of a Rat in the North corner of the house, or in the Sheep direction of Southwest.

5. Seasonal Trinity

Another grouping of animal signs creates the four seasonal trinity combinations that bring the luck of seasonal abundance. To many astrology experts, this is regarded as one of the most powerful combinations, and when it exists within a family made up of either parent or both parents) and with one or more children, it indicates that, collectively these family members are strong enough to transform all negative luck indications for the family members that make up the combination for the entire year. Thus when the annual indications of the year are not favorable, the existence of the seasonal combination of animal signs in any living abode can transform the bad luck into better luck especially during the season indicated by the combination.

All three signs must live together in the same house or be in the same office working in close proximity for this powerful pattern to work well. For greater impact, it is better feng shui if they are all using the direction associated with the relevant seasons. The table below summarises the Seasonal groupings.

The Sheep belongs to the seasonal combination of Summer, a combination which strengthens its links with the Snake and the Horse. Should a Sheep and Horse marry, and they have a Snake child, the three will create the trinity of summer. With the trinity created, they attract the luck of abundance during the summer season! This means that they are not only exceptionally close, but also attract the luck of the great summer harvest during the summer season!

SEASONAL TRINITIES OF THE HOROSCOPE

ANIMAL SIGNS	SEASON	ELEMENT	DIRECTION
Dragon, Rabbit, Tiger	Spring	Wood	East
Snake, Horse, Sheep	**Summer**	**Fire**	**South**
Monkey, Rooster, Dog	Autumn	Metal	West
Ox, Rat, Boar	Winter	Water	North

SHEEP WITH RAT
Sheep makes romantic overtures and Rat responds

Big thinking Rat falls for seductive Sheep who is in its element in 2011. The Sheep guy is extremely attractive, being the strong silent type who hooks the Rat lady in without the latter even realising what is happening. As for the Sheep lady, she is at her sensuous best and will have an aura of magnetism about her that Rat will find very hard to pin down. As a result, this is a year when Rat will find Sheep hard to resist.

Unlike last year when both found the year of the Tiger very trying indeed, in 2011, the new set of energies re-energizes Sheep's libido and galvanises Rat into action. Rat enjoys the double Big Auspicious, while Sheep stays beautifully romantic yet still down-to-earth, making her irresistible. Sheep is one of two signs that lives in the matriarchal corner of Southwest. When the peach blossom star of 4 enters the SW, romantic tendencies get enhanced.

When Sheep gets involved with Rat, it is likely that your romance can easily turn serious. In 2011, any kind of love relationship has more than an even chance to blossom and lead to more serious commitment. Marriage between the two is more than possible. Rat this year who has been going out with Sheep or who has been married to one will start to see Sheep in a new light, so that although the psychic aura around Sheep is still lacklustre, the romance star brings another kind of brightness into the relationship.

The couple that comprises the 27 year old Wood Rat and the 20 year old Metal Sheep is not as good as the other pairings, but in 2011, their energies are less in discord. If they can allow love to flow freely between them instead of trying to change one another too much, the union has a chance. Otherwise, if quarrels get in the way, it is better not to get too involved.

In Chinese astrological circles, Rat is renowned for its flirtatious tendencies while Sheep is shy and understated. Their personalities could not be more different. Better for Rat to resist Sheep (who is terribly desirable this year) than risk an unhappy commitment. Over the longer term, this is not an ideal pairing. For the 27 year old Wood Rat and the 32 year old Earth Sheep, the relationship does not at first look promising, but as the year moves on, attraction between the two intensifies. For the 39 year old Water Rat and the 32 year old Earth Sheep both enjoy better luck, so the relationship is more stable.

SHEEP WITH OX
Ox is attracted to Sheep's loving nature

Surprisingly, the year turns out to be rather amiable for this pair as Ox is attracted to Sheep's loving nature. This is an unlikely match as Ox and Sheep have little in common and in fact can even find each other rather boring. Where Ox tends to be calculating and quantitative, Sheep tends to be artistic and creative.

> While they are not exactly opposites in character and tenacity, they are like the yin and yang of couples; when they get along, they complement each other beautifully, but it takes quite a bit of seeing each other for real affection to grow between them.

In Chinese astrology, Ox and Sheep are considered to be adversaries with no time for each other. If anything, there is usually a turning away rather than a gravitating to one another. Should they become a couple, it is likely there must be some special circumstances bringing them together.

This is not a relationship that can be ignited by a sudden spark of passion. There is unlikely to be instant attraction between them. But in 2011 however, their energies appear to be happily compatible. It is a year when Sheep is feeling romantic and seductive, and in this frame of mind, Sheep can be very attractive, even irresistible. Ox is in an expansive mood this year and it is a time when falling for someone becomes something easy to do. Unlike the cosmic forces of last year, the new pattern of energies seems to be generating clashes at the macro level, yet at the micro levels of personal relationships, there is more loving and a tendency for more bonding to take place. Maybe this is why even astrological enemies can find each other madly attractive.

Instead of arguing with each other, and one finding the other aggravating and annoying, there is instead a loving kind of cosmic chi. Both sides become more accepting of one another's shortcomings.

But as to whether the whole relationship can last very long, it is unlikely that the same level of loving energy can be maintained beyond this year and next. Those living together either in matrimony or as a partnership will find the year a lot less stressful than previous years. There continues to be insensitivity in the relationship but a lot less so. This is a good year to sink all your differences and rekindle some of the passion lost in the intervening years.

SHEEP WITH TIGER
Heaven & Earth chi bring them together

This year Tiger discovers qualities in Sheep it
was previously blind to. In 2011 there are cosmic
connections between these two signs; a powerful yin
and yang type bonding that manifests heaven and
earth influences. This acts like a magnet for this pair
drawing them close in spite of whatever differences or
reservations they may each have.

Those married to each other will find the fires get lit
again by cosmic connections. It is a good year for them
as a couple. This is a year when they find themselves
strongly motivated by each other. This can be a most
powerful aphrodisiac. It is uncanny to see Tiger and
Sheep cavorting together lost in one another's presence
and actually finding joy being in each other's company,
when in most years these are signs that would ordinarily
have little interest in each other.

They do not have much in common; their interests
could not be further apart, and personality-wise, they
do not even enjoy complementary skills or attitudes.
There is little that could be the basis for a rock-solid
relationship. Yet in 2011, real love and affection sparks
up between Tiger and Sheep, fuelled principally by
Sheep's peach blossom star influence. In the light of this

powerful star and given Tiger's Heaven Seal connecting with Sheep's Earth Seal, these two signs will basically be blind to anything other than their attraction and the respect they inspire in each other.

> In 2011, this will be an emotional relationship. It will have little to do with the head or any careful thinking. The Tiger person will find Sheep's conservative nature quaint, even attractive.

Should these two signs be married, it is likely that Tiger will be older than Sheep, and this works well. A match between the 61 year old Tiger would work well with the 32 year old Earth Sheep, and the 49 year old Water Tiger might go for the 20 year old Metal Sheep.

This has to do with the elements with Sheep's element "producing" Tiger's element! All other age pairings work as well, because the winds that blow to them are so complementary and in harmony.

Both Tiger and Sheep are up to being amiable and sociable this year. They are in a loving mood, so there will be no confrontations to spoil the pretty picture they make.

SHEEP WITH RABBIT
Allies in need of yang chi create their own

In 2011, Rabbit turns to its ally the Sheep for
support and a strong shoulder and the Sheep does
not disappoint. Here, the astrological affinity between
these two signs ignites goodwill and encouragement,
and Sheep, whose energy is both loving and giving in
2011, will shore up its friend and ally, the Rabbit.

Rabbit has a troubled year filled with countless things
going awry, while Sheep enjoys brand new Earth Seal
energy, which is both invigorating and inspiring. Sheep
is also very creative, being bitten by the intellectual
and entrepreneurial bug. And since Sheep can be big
hearted by nature, there is more than enough room in
its mandala to offer space to its astrological ally.

As a result, Rabbit responds with grace and vivacity,
rolling up its sleeves and falling in with the energy of
the Sheep. Together they create a new brand of yang
chi, which opens new vistas and doorways for both.
This is a mutually satisfying relationship in 2011, for
one brings out the best in the other.

They will get high indulging in the same things, so
a natural compatibility starts to unfold for them;
an awareness of the artistic and creative flair they

generate together. This brings them happiness and for the Rabbit, it is both comforting and nurturing. In essence, this is what love is about. The more Sheep lends Rabbit an ear and a shoulder for support, the more they become soulmates, so 2011 becomes then a good binding year. Trust develops between the pair and this itself is usually strong enough for them both to transform negative energies into good.

They become comfortable looking out for each other, and then a quiet rapport and sense of comradeship develops. In 2011, Sheep's restful energy and Rabbit's resilience continues to generate sweet resonance; so despite it being a rather tough year for Rabbit, as a pair, they overcome bad vibes to create their own yang-drenched sanctuary.

Any problems that may surface between them will be due to Rabbit's afflictive state in 2011, being hit by the *wu wang* or five yellow. This is the star of misfortune and it is usually associated with a variety of ills including problems in relationships, ill health and a vulnerability to misunderstandings and quarrels. The *wu wang* brings all sorts of unexpected problems to the Rabbit but this can be overcome.

SHEEP WITH DRAGON
Good but unlikely to go deep

Dragon does not have very much in common with Sheep, but in 2011, they can establish an amiable and friendly relationship. They do not need to go very deep with one another, and in fact, it benefits them both to be this way. In the case of this couple, superficiality has its advantages. Better to connect well at surface levels than discover things about one another that just do not fit well.

In 2011, Sheep is very grounded and down-to-earth; Sheep is also having its eye on achieving big things, yet romance is also very much part of its psyche this year. Thus despite wanting to focus strongly on work, career and making it big in business, nevertheless, Sheep is also keeping an eye out for the big romance! This arises from the feng shui winds of the year creating the energy of love relationships in the mind of Sheep.

Dragon will respond to Sheep because the chi energy of these two signs are complementing each other very well indeed. Here we see the influence of heaven and earth casting a benevolent influence, and even though these two signs may not wish to connect at deeper levels, still they will find enjoyment and passion with one another.

It is one of Sheep's strengths that in the Zodiac pantheon of the 12 signs, it has the greatest ability to attract and keep love relationships. Sheep is able to win over whoever it sets its sights on. In 2011, Sheep is influenced by the star of romance, and should someone of the Sheep sign cast eyes on Dragon, there is little Dragon can do but succumb. The Chinese also believe that Sheep has the most effective way of connecting with people in power, so they have the best potential when it comes to exerting their subtle influence on other people's emotions.

> For Dragon to get together with Sheep has special benefits in 2011; the feng shui chart reveals a beneficial alliance arising from the complementarities of the feng shui winds of both signs. They create advantageous completion luck that benefits them both.

They both gain equally from doing things together, lending energy and support. Those of you who are married to each other would be well advised to take advantage of these good winds to do something meaningful together, for instance, have a baby, move into a new house; celebrate with a holiday together or start a new project.

SHEEP WITH SNAKE
Suppressed animosity between these two

The 2011 distribution of chi energy around the Zodiac cycle repeats the scenario of last year for this pair; Snake's vitality is at its zenith, while Sheep's energy is at a low ebb. One is all fired up, eager to savor life and start new adventures; the other is distracted, limiting its attention almost exclusively to its own inner world. This is a mismatched pair having their own hidden agendas, and whatever animosity simmers beneath could well get unstuck and rise up into the open. Not a good thing to happen!

> It is hard for these two signs to find common ground in 2011 mainly because of the way the winds are blowing; there are different aspirations pulling them apart. While Snake is feeling adventurous and optimistic, Sheep is coming to terms with its own feelings of inadequacy.

Energy, rhythm and even their pace of thinking is at odds. So if you are getting together for the first time, better to find comfort and love elsewhere. Snake may be feeling passionate but simpering emotional-type romancing is not what Snake wants. Sheep is feeling sentimental and romantic, quite unlike Snake, so their views of love and romance are different.

There is little to pull these two together; even if they did have something in common on which to build a potentially satisfying relationship, it is unlikely to last. Both signs get turned off when bored, and both get bored easily. Snake tends to be intellectually snobbish while Sheep is materialistic. They respect different skills and strengths, and if they live together, it is sure to permeate and spoil their relationship

The older of the two signs probably has the patience to live through their relationship if they happen to be married. The 68 year old Water Sheep for instance, though suffering from failing health, will be tolerant and indulgent of its Snake partner. But the Metal Sheep cannot be bothered.

From the viewpoint of Snake, those in their forties, fifties and sixties who are married - the Wood, Water and Fire Snake - will simply not hesitate to fool around and cultivate outside love interests. Suspicions, frustrations and repressed anger cause aggravations of this couple. But Sheep is as likely to succumb to outside temptations. So unless there is an understanding between this pair, it seems better to create their own private worlds away from each other.

SHEEP WITH HORSE
Excellent match with real affection

Horse and Sheep are soulmates and secret friends who communicate at a very special level of understanding. There is real affection between them and irrespective of how any year pans out for them, together they always hold strong.

Their connection transcends time and space and together they can both achieve anything they set their minds to. External setbacks and difficulties cannot put any dents in your relationship so really you have great compatibility. They are stronger when together and this means more to them than anything else. Theirs is one of the most favorable of the Zodiac matches.

In 2011, Horse enjoys a year filled with vitality. There is the promise of success and more money for Horse. Sheep is getting over the difficulties of the past year and in 2011 is entering into a nesting time when thoughts turn to love and romance, marriage and babies. Those not married will want to tie the knot this year and it will be good to do so. Those already married will be thinking of making babies and of course, having a Rabbit child would be very auspicious for Sheep. Happily, Horse is going through a good year marked by strong energy and inner assurance. This makes it easy for Sheep's needs to resonate very positively with Horse. Horse and Sheep are not just secret friends, they also share the same Zodiac house of sexuality and passion, with Horse exuding the male yang energy and Sheep creating the female yin energy. These astrological indications suggest a good level of sexual chemistry between them, and with Sheep being influenced by the peach blossom star this year, this pair will take their love to very high levels of satisfaction. For them, romance is a meaningful word.

The year will be meaningful for them both, and for those in their thirties, this could be a breakthrough year that sees their collective asset wealth growing. There is success in what they are putting together and commercial enterprises started by either should have a good chance of success with the support of the other.

The married pair should know that the effect of their synergy will open many profitable pathways for them. Working together generates a special kind of energy and this enhances the vital cosmic chi that brings success to everything they do. Look for gemstones to activate your lucky planets to help you reach even higher levels of success.

SHEEP WITH SHEEP
Their similarities keep them together

Sheep is very grounded in 2011, thinking and making decisions with a clarity and a focus that is the envy of its Zodiac friends and allies! When the two of you get together in a love relationship, you become so sensible and practical it can almost take all the romance out of your relationship.

And yet, 2011 is also a year when the star number of peach blossom - which awakens the romantic inside you - flies to the Southwest, which is of course your direction. So it puts you the Sheep in a very nesting kind of mood. It softens you, makes you mellow and incites the passion that lies latent most of the time. In this year of the Rabbit however, Sheep will give in to its amorous feelings, so here we are seeing a renewed and energized Sheep.

Those not already married will want to put down roots this year. The urge to set up house, start a family and create a family unit is simply too strong to resist. You will find the question of commitment on your mind a lot, so a Sheep going out with another Sheep will happily be thinking alike here. Happiness is definitely on the cards - a double happiness event such as a marriage!

For those of you already married, this is a year when the thought of babies is definitely very real. And with it being the year of the Rabbit, your ally, this only makes the timing all the better! So it is likely then that family and everything this entails is very much on both your minds. Here we see also the potential for yet another double happiness event happening. Must be the influence of the love star which is also very family-oriented in its positive influences.

> The great thing is that you are both thinking alike. That's what's so good about your relationship. Here it is not about compatibility so much as it is about wanting the same things. Note that your practical side is also being activated and this brings out all the organisational skills and yes, almost matriarchal energies within you.

You will both be very down-to-earth in 2011, and the woman in the relationship of a Sheep-Sheep couple will take charge, setting the tone and rhythm of developments for the year.

SHEEP WITH MONKEY
Not especially good in 2011

The Sheep and Monkey do not really have too much in common in 2011. Sheep will feel an aversion for Monkey simply because there is the whiff of yin chi coming from Monkey, a sense of negativity which somehow puts Sheep off. Sheep will come to the conclusion that cheeky and unfaithful Monkey is not good for its peace of mind.

Monkey is less than enchanted by Sheep's attitude to life and living. Monkey finds Sheep's values and aspirations boring and almost narcissistic, so there is very little compatibility here. It will not take long for either side to develop an aversion and turn away from each other. Whatever attraction there is will not last long as both sides soon tire of one another.

Sheep and Monkey harbor their own suspicions about the other's motives. It seems so hard for this pair to engender any kind of trust, and in a meeting of the younger representatives of these two signs, there will be more confusion and bafflement than love. Two singles meeting one another for the first time will find it hard for any sparks to ignite; they simply cannot get very far in a love relationship.

It is possible that both will be feeling amorous, as both these signs come under the direct influence of the star of peach blossom. Romance is definitely on both their minds, but the problem is that romance finds it hard to kindle between this pair. Maybe all there is in the relationship is purely physical - passion and lust - and following up on that, little more. Both find it hard to develop deeper feelings.

In a marriage between this pair, it is likely that the magic has long since lain dormant. And it is unlikely that 2011 is the year to get the flames soaring again. This should not be too surprising as these two signs have little in common, with an approach to life that stands at opposite ends of the great divide. Personality-wise they are very different, and neither is attracted to the other for very long.

Monkey is a strong sign while Sheep tends to be soft-spoken and gentle. There is a powerful vitality emanating from Monkey's aura, while Sheep prefers to come across more sensitive. Monkey is simply unable to read Sheep's moods. It is really much better for this pair not to get involved with one another, and those married to try not to get in each other's way in 2011.

SHEEP WITH ROOSTER
Good rapport but perhaps not this year

The Sheep and Rooster tend to be very wary with each
other when they have any kind of close relationship.
Between them is a distance that makes it hard for
them to really connect. In a love relationship, whatever
passion ignited will be tinged with an element of
uncertainty, as a result of which, this is not a couple
that can really reach great heights of compatibility.

These two signs generally try to avoid each other. It
is an instinctive reaction which neither gives much
thought to really, but should Sheep get romantically
involved with Rooster in 2011, the pairing could well
work, but only for a little while.

There might be initial attraction, but don't be fooled;
whatever is ignited will soon dissipate. Whatever good
rapport between you during the first few meetings
is unlikely to last as Sheep will tire of Rooster's
distracted attitude towards their relationship. This
is simply not the kind of year to engage Rooster in
any kind of love run-around, as 2011 tends to be
challenging for the bird sign. Many things apart from
romance are on its mind, so to Sheep who is dancing
lightly through a year when romance is all-important,
there is simply no compatibility here. The problem also

is that Sheep tends to be slightly in awe of Rooster and is put off by Rooster's tendency to be brusque and abrupt, attributes that will be very much in evidence through 2011. Sheep is a gentle soft-spoken sort of person and Rooster's strong and loud presence is definitely intimidating and not in a nice way. In 2011 Rooster is coping with its own set of problems, so it is likely to come across bossy and moody.

At best, Sheep can have only a superficial friendship with Rooster. Should these two marry, hostility and resentment is sure to creep into the relationship. The problem also lies in Sheep not being in sync with Rooster's long term plans and ambitions. So the way they think and address the year will be different to the point of being painful. Far better that they stay off the subject of building anything together.

If married, Rooster's eyes could stray, and Sheep too could look elsewhere for solace and comfort. Its peach blossom influence will likely point it in this direction, so in this pairing there is no guarantee of fidelity. The good news is that infidelity does not bring a level of heartbreak that is unbearable for either of them. They will deal with their marriage problems by being prepared to close one eye to indiscretions.

SHEEP WITH DOG
Can find companionship and love

Sheep has love in its viewfinder in 2011 and Dog is both attractive and extremely willing as well, so this is a year when notions of romance between this pair can take root, grow and blossom. As with last year, sparks are sure to ignite between this pair, except that in 2011 the fires of love tend to burn stronger. And it is the kind that can lead to something more permanent too.

> Sheep and Dog are extremely compatible this year, finding an easy familiarity and a natural leaning towards each other. These are two of the Zodiac's more gentle and caring signs; they are loyal and nurturing towards those they love. For them, love grows slowly but surely, and once committed, they tend to be faithful and trusting.

This pair is thus happy to gravitate towards each other, and then end up having eyes only for each other. It is a very happy situation, one that is not to be taken for granted.

Relationships like this can be hard to find and develop, and for both, the year helps you along. Dog especially is enjoying the support of the great power of 8, which brings good vibes - relationships tend to proceed smoothly this year and with Sheep being so grounded and practical in 2011, all signs look very promising. Those of you involved in a relationship as an eager Sheep or a willing Dog would do well to cherish the love you have for one another. This is a great year to create a commitment towards one another.

The Sheep and Dog are not stubborn people and they are rarely quick to anger. They are easy going and sensitive, so this can be a very nice and stable bond that can stand the test of time. But for those already married to one another however, do not expect that what you need is grand passion. Yours is a steady, stable and solid kind of togetherness, and not the loud intense kind of excitement. You are two people who prefer unwavering loyalty to flamboyant fervor.

So in both a love or work relationship, this couple pairs well. But if you are hoping to have an affair of the heart or be engaging in some kind of illicit relationship, it is doomed from the start, because you are simply not the kind of people who are made that way. For both of you, Sheep and Dog, love must mean commitment; it is not a passionate fling you can just walk away from.

SHEEP WITH BOAR
Finding Happiness & Humor

The Sheep the Boar are very well suited and compatible, and those of you involved with each other will be certain to feel all the benefits of getting together in what looks like being a great year for you.

> As a pair or individually, 2011 brings some wonderful new highs for Sheep and also for Boar. For the latter especially, blessed by the power of 8 and also receiving goodies from the 24 mountain stars constellation, 2011 is a year brimming with good vibrations.

For Sheep, in a year when notions of romance come to the fore and when marriage and family take priority in your consciousness, getting together with an ally will make your cup runneth over. Happiness is on the cards for you, and satisfaction as well.

As allies, the year works even better, and you will see that as a couple, your bonded energies can transcend everything. You have such affinity that you can anticipate each other's needs. You sense each other's discomforts instinctively, so here the empathy and feelings go beyond skin-deep. The good news then is that you are entering into a year which smiles at you.

There is sunshine energy enveloping you both. Life shines brightly and auspiciously for you.

Those already married can engage in all the meaningful fun aspects of building a life and family together - have babies, buy a house, celebrate an anniversary ... undertaking any of these projects will bring joyousness and satisfaction - and they will also bring a great deal of beneficial yang energy as well.

Yours is a partnership that works with little effort, so do make the most of it. Boar must be alert to the possibility of something very meaningful coming its way - this will be something that enhances your net worth. Sheep will help make the most of whatever comes because Sheep is grounded, practical and extremely insightful this year, blessed by the star of the Earth Seal. There is great strength and synergy in your being together. In 2011, it will be very easy for you to reach new highs in your relationship with each other, utilising not only your own intrinsic energies and compatibility, but also harnessing the trust and bonding aspirations that flow freely between you. You are sure then to grow stronger this year, fuelled by auspicious feng shui winds.

Sheep's Monthly Horoscope 2011

Sheep Continually Distracted by Matters of the Heart

This year, Sheep is under the strong influence of the Peach Blossom star, causing Sheep to focus on love, relationships and family. Work tends to take a back seat unless it involves loved ones. While the Sheep who works from home will thrive in 2011, those in big corporate jobs that constantly take it away from the family will feel the strain. Romance luck blossoms and the single Sheep could find its soulmate this year. Married Sheep on the other hand will be feeling needy and if your spouse does not give you the attention you need, there is danger of straying outside the marriage. As for wealth, try and capture money-making opportunities during months that favor you; wealth luck on the whole is average this year unless you can catch the odd wave of good fortune that comes your way. The good news is you are brought the luck of Big Auspicious from your secret friend the Horse, so try not to miss the boat; this could indeed be the year of your big break!

1 ST MONTH
February 4th - March 5th 2011

OVERCOMING EMOTIONAL PROBLEMS

The year starts off difficult with the misfortune star paying a visit. Combining with the relationship star in your chart, it causes problems of an emotional kind. You are likely to feel pulled in many different directions, leaving you unsure what decisions to take and who to side. Friendships and family ties are strained when outside influences enter the picture. Remember that blood is thicker than water, and long-time friendships count for something. Don't let the lure of excitement cloud your judgment, causing you to make a decision you'll regret. Keep your feet firmly on the ground and make use of your Earth Seal energy by carrying the **Earth Seal amulet**. This will help you stay strong amidst persuasive influence and help you make sensible and beneficial decisions.

Carry the **Earth Seal amulet** to keep you grounded and to help ensure you make decisions that are beneficial in the longer term.

WORK & CAREER - *Keep a Low Profile*

This is a time to stay low profile in your job. While you need to continue working efficiently and well, this is not a time when new ideas will be well received. Don't try to be too creative this month. This is not a time to show the genius side of you. Be a good worker, deliver the results but avoid adopting a do-or-die attitude, for it will more likely be the latter this month. Steer clear of making big decisions this month, as they are likely to be tainted with negative chi. Delay any important judgment calls till later. If you are unhappy about something in your job, you may have to live with it for a while. This is no time to be complaining about peripheral matters. Fighting small battles and winning them, only to lose the war, will lead to tears and regrets later.

BUSINESS - *Proceed Cautiously*

Things may be slow this month when it comes to new business opportunities. Although you won't be short on offers on the table, it is better to proceed cautiously. There may be some deals that appear too good to be true. You may attract some shady characters into your life and it may not be easy to spot who is and who isn't a fraud. To play it safe, wait till next month before putting out money or investing in something that carries the element of risk. This month the energies in your chart are tainted by the misfortune star, so stay low profile to ensure you don't fall victim to it.

LOVE & RELATIONSHIPS – *Be Careful*
Tread carefully when it comes to love and new relationships this month. Those of you who are still single should take things a little slow. Jumping into something you are not ready for could lead to a broken heart, or worse, real danger. Wait till the chi energy settles before taking things to another level. By all means go out and have some fun, but beware leading anyone on, or appearing to be more serious than you are. Your admirer may not take everything quite so lightly. For those of you who are married, watch you don't fall for outside temptation. There is danger of heartache from infidelity. Protect your marriage by wearing the **double happiness** symbol.

EDUCATION – *Some Obstacles*
You can expect some obstacles to crop up this month. Academically you will be coping well, but there could be some grievances when it comes to friendships and your relationships with your peers. Don't let yourself get distracted by matters of the heart. If you're serious about your studies, the advice is not to get too heavily involved when it comes to romance just yet. Leave that for much later on.

2ND MONTH
March 6th - April 4th 2011

ROMANTIC PURSUITS KEEP YOU ON A HIGH

Expect an intensive month ahead when things happen quickly. The energies are extremely powerful in your chart right now and it is all about seizing opportunities and making the best of them. If your attitude is right, you will find yourself ready for any challenge that is thrust your way. The more proactive you are this month, the more positive the outcomes of your endeavors. Work will be more research-oriented in nature and the more widely read you are, the more you will be able to capitalize on your particular situation. Your financial situation is comfortable, but do not overspend. There is some danger of excess, so temper your penchant for the creature comforts of life this month. Those in the mood for love can expect a roller coaster of a ride, but do not get embroiled in illicit affairs, which will backfire very quickly.

WORK & CAREER - *Creative*

You are buzzing with creative ideas this month. You won't always feel this inspired, so when you are, don't let them fall by the wayside. Use your originality this month to show what a star you are. You have the potential to rise up very high in whatever career path you have chosen for yourself. If you've been working for years in your particular field of expertise, this could be a turning point when you discover why you were meant to do what you're doing.

BUSINESS - *Exciting Times!*

Make the most of your ability to get along with others to further your business goals this month. You will find that successful networking brings incredible opportunities, sometimes quite unexpected ones. Don't underestimate what a particular someone can do for you. This is a time when you cannot judge a book by its cover. There are treasures under the surface of recently-met acquaintances that could prove distinctly important to you in the near future. This may be your chance to enter into an exciting partnership of some kind. If there are any formal agreements to be signed, try to sign before the month is up. Your luck is blazing bright this month, but the luck of benefiting from strategic alliances fades when next month dawns.

LOVE & RELATIONSHIPS - *Hot Pursuit*

Whether you're looking for fun or something more serious, the potential is there. Romantic pursuits bring much excitement into your life right now if you'll let it. Be sure to be out and about town if you are single and eligible. You meet love luck on both ends of the stick. While you may be pursuing someone of interest, don't be surprised if others are pursuing you. They may not be one and the same, but there is nothing wrong in enjoying all the attention. Boost Peach Blossom luck by placing a Rat, your Peach Blossom animal, in the North of your bedroom. This will help those of you looking for someone you can develop a longer term relationship with.

FRIENDSHIP – *Good Friends*

Friendships will feature prominently in your life right now. You find relationships with your closest friends taking up a lot of your time, but they will also be good for you. If the opportunity arises to help someone, be happy you are in a position to assist. Don't turn down someone's request for help. If you can genuinely lend a hand, you will be building up your store of good karma, and at a time when you will truly enjoy doing it.

EDUCATION – *Productive*

A productive month awaits the student Sheep. You have the potential to achieve top grades so don't let anything or anyone hold you back. This is a time when belief in yourself can conquer just about anything. Work hard now and make your good study luck count.

3RD MONTH
April 5th - May 5th 2011

A MONTH OF MISUNDERSTANDINGS

The jubilant energies of last month come to an end this month, when your life will instead be peppered by misunderstandings in relationships, both personal and professional. Your mood changes because new aggravations crop up to make you irritable, worried or depressed. You may find yourself placing too much emphasis on what others think of you. Don't ask for the opinions of others too much this month; you may not like what you hear and it may affect you in a manner you're not emotionally ready to cope with. Try to rely more on your own sense of self worth. Have faith in your own abilities. Even if others may not seem to appreciate you, don't start feeling sorry for yourself. There is no need to justify yourself to anybody.

WORK & CAREER - *Hold Your Temper*

The quarrelsome star wields its influence this month, making you irritable and difficult to deal with. Little things send you flying off the handle. Particularly if you're working for somebody else, there is only so much you can get away with, so refrain from letting your fury loose if you don't want to lose out or worse, lose your job! Working with others will prove tougher than usual this month. When given a choice, it is probably best for you to tackle solo projects than to work as an integral team player. Beware also of office politics this month. Display a **Rooster figurine** on your desk to protect against this kind of bad luck. Try not to make mistakes by being more diligent. There are enemies waiting for you to slip up. Avoid getting into arguments over small things. If there are great differences in opinion, don't try to come to a compromise. Either give in or settle it next month.

BUSINESS – *Lie Low*

This month it is better to lie low. Do not invest big amounts of money. Avoid risky ventures. It may even be a good idea to take a vacation and go away for a while. Your relationships with others tend to be strained this month, particularly when there are issues involving money. Your fuse is shorter than usual and this could cause you to be unpleasant

Display a Rooster on your desk
at work this month to protect
against office politics.

to deal with. Avoid making small talk, which could lead to the wrong things being said.

LOVE & RELATIONSHIPS - *Keep Things Simple*
Try and keep things simple in your love relationships. Don't force your partner to dwell on your personal miseries with you; you may not like their responses or opinions, and you certainly don't need another reason to quarrel. At the same time, try and keep your opinions to yourself. Although you may mean something as a compliment, it may be taken the wrong way. Avoid sensitive subjects and don't poke fun at your partner; your sense of humor may be taken the wrong way.

EDUCATION - *Play by the Rules*
Beware of trouble with the authorities this month. Stick to the rules because bending them even ever so slightly this month won't see you getting away with it. If you've been skiving off class or if you've not been entirely honest when preparing your assignments, this month you could well get caught out. Your relationships with others may be strained in the next four weeks. Don't expect total loyalty from your buddies. It's every man for himself. If you're going to stand a chance, it may help if you start thinking that way too.

4TH MONTH
May 6th - June 5th 2011

FALLING SICK AND FEELING WEAK

You're afflicted by the illness energies of the month, so although luck may be quite good when it comes to work and money matters, you will be slowed down somewhat by health concerns. Don't take poor health lightly; a minor ailment could develop into something more serious. Although you may have some crucial deadlines to meet that require keeping some unconventional hours, don't make a habit of it or your health is bound to suffer. Get enough exercise and eat well. To protect against illness stars this month wear plenty of gold jewellery as this has the powerful effect of warding off illness chi.

WORK & CAREER – *Health Obstacles*

Career luck is good but obstacles arise in the form of poor health and flagging energy. If you have to take sick days off work, you could miss out on some opportunities that would otherwise be yours. You may be handpicked to head a new project but it is your health that threatens to jeopardize this opportunity. Wear or carry a **Wu Lou** amulet to protect against falling sick and avoid sitting in a Southwest location. Don't make yourself to concentrate for too long without breaks. Take a short walk if you find your attentiveness ebbing. Keep your efforts short and sharp. When your mind is tired, go home and start again the next day. You have potential to produce very good work this month if you manage your mental and physical strength well.

BUSINESS – *Make Use of the Team*
For those of you at helm of your own business, your ability to motivate your staff gets enhanced this month. Productivity will increase more from good management than from personal effort. While you may have good ideas and an excellent strategic mind, don't dismiss what others can contribute to the success of the business. Focus on bringing out the best in what your team can offer. Holding focused management meetings will give renewed direction to your business.

LOVE & RELATIONSHIPS – *A Time to Bond*
Time spent building your relationship with your partner will be time well spent this month. This is a time when you can discover plenty you didn't know about your partner and this will only serve to bring the two of you closer to one another. Sheep who are settling down into their nesting period will find the

idea of starting a family very appealing. Don't avoid discussing the future with your partner. If you have been seeing each other with no talk of settling down, you may want to raise the subject if it concerns you.

Those of you who are still single will find this month great in terms of romance. You can charm just about anyone with your playful personality. While you won't be short of admirers, this could be the right time to settle on a special someone. Focusing on building a real relationship will probably give you more joy than casual dating right now.

EDUCATION - Strike a Balance

Things go smoothly with college when it comes to your studies, but watch you're not spending too much time cooped up indoors with your head in your books. Balance your work time with enough time off to relax. This way your mind will stay fresher and you'll find you do even better. You *can* work too hard, so use that as a good excuse to recharge your batteries when you're feeling burnt out.

5TH MONTH
June 6th - July 6th 2011

WINNING AND ACHIEVING GOALS

This is an incredibly lucky month for those born in Sheep years. The stars in your chart are aligned in your favor and you will have both opportunities come your way, as well as the means to benefit from them. You're in your element so make the most of this auspicious time. Signs point to a major change in your life. It could be a shift in your mindset or a more tangible change like a change in job, a change in residence or even a relocation. But the mood of the month is a buoyant one. As long as you embrace whatever comes your way with the right attitude, you're likely to do very well indeed. Recognize when someone is trying to help you. Don't push aside suggestions from family and loved ones; used the right way, these suggestions could be just what you need to propel you to the next level of whatever it is you are working on.

WORK & CAREER - *Be Courageous*

Those of you with ambitions to make it big in your career will find this month a fulfilling one. This is a time when you can pursue lofty goals with confidence.

Although getting what you want may involve a change of lifestyle, you will be able to work things out in the end, so be courageous. When contemplating a major decision, give yourself some time to think things over carefully. By all means take counsel from your family and others who may be equally affected by whatever decision you ultimately choose to take. Once you've made up your mind, ride with it without looking back. Your luck is optimal right now, so don't worry too much about making the wrong choice. If you feel good about something, go for it.

BUSINESS – *Hooking Up with the Right People*
Growth luck is good this month, and anything you start now will have every chance of success. Don't be averse to taking on partners. Hooking up with the right people will allow you to expand exceptionally quickly. Turn your attention to some of the relationships you have recently forged. There could be a goldmine to be tapped, and if you can work out a mutually beneficial arrangement, it could be a partnership that brings both success and much personal satisfaction and joy. Make your work a passion; if you have your heart in whatever you are doing, you'll do it exponentially better. For those of you who have reached the end of the road in what you've been doing, this could be the time to think

about making a major change in your life. Don't be afraid to take big steps. A major change in direction could be scary in the short term, but it could turn out to be the best decision you've made when looked at from a longer term perspective.

LOVE & RELATIONSHIPS - *Deep Connection*

Those single among you will have no shortage of suitors this month, but the time may have come to pick your someone special. Don't feel pressurized into say yes to a steady relationship, but if the person is right for you, in your heart you will know. If you're already in a steady relationship, your connection with your partner is likely to grow stronger in the coming weeks. You may find that love and business go hand in hand this month, so it will not be surprising if you end up meeting someone in the course of your work.

EDUCATION - *A Prolific Time*

The month is one of prolific study energy, making academic work a breeze for Sheep students. If you are successfully focusing your attention on your work, you should be reaping real rewards. Those of you attempting to win scholarships will do well if you submit their application this month. Exam luck is also good and it will be easy to achieve the grades you are aiming for.

6TH MONTH
July 7th - Aug 7th 2011

A GOOD MONTH TO FOCUS ON WORK

A fast-paced month when career and business luck is good. Friends and allies surround you with goodwill and assistance, and word of mouth leads to recognition from influential people. This is a good time to focus on work and making money. Many opportunities come your way and many of them very exciting ones. Watch however you don't let your health suffer while going after the big time. When exhaustion sets in, you could find yourself making careless mistakes, some of which may prove to be quite costly. Pace yourself and don't bite off more than you can chew. Make the best use of your allies and don't be greedy about sharing the pie. Make best use of your resources and you'll end up gaining more in the end.

WORK & CAREER – *Taking a Higher Profile*

You're bursting with energy this month. You start to take a higher profile at work and become firmly entrenched as a core member of the team. This brings new possibilities to your career path. This is a turning point month when you could suddenly realize how lucky you are to be doing what you are doing. Your increased input into the strategic side of things will motivate you to even greater heights. While your take home pay may not have risen to reflect the additional effort you are putting into your work, what matters is you are making very tangible progress. You will be rewarded in time, but for now, don't get greedy. The more you give, the more you get back. Just be patient.

BUSINESS - *Marketing Efforts Pay Off*

Fire energy is strong in your chart this month. Thus getting the right publicity and media attention holds much promise for your business right now. This is a good month to launch an advertising campaign and to actively raise the awareness for your company and your product. Be sure to be actively involved in the conceptualization of any ad campaign. You want it branded with your touch and more importantly, your auspicious chi this month.

Not every idea you put out there will work. If you start down one path and find it not pulling in the returns you expect, change course. Things are happening quickly and some mistakes will be made, but as long as you don't dwell on them and stay nimble on your feet, you will make more good than bad judgment calls. Stay focused, stay creative and stay confident. This is a fabulous month and things will only get better as they year rolls forward.

LOVE & RELATIONSHIPS - *Simmering*

The vigorous Fire energy in your chart fuels a hidden passion simmering beneath the surface and a lot of you secretly harbor the wish for some real adventurism when it comes to love and relationships. But if you succumb to your desires, it could either bring you a lot of happiness and satisfaction, or it could cause you a lot of trouble. Remember to keep your head when playing the love game. Matters of the heart are not to be taken lightly, and the Sheep person is feeling rather emotional this year, where it doesn't take much to make you feel extremely elated or devastatingly depressed. Don't wear your heart on your sleeve. Remember to keep a balance in your life and don't let your relationships rule you. Staying strong and dispassionate to a certain degree will only help you this month.

EDUCATION - *Busy like a Bee*

A busy month full of activities awaits you. There are countless things you'd like to pursue and the only thing stopping you are the limited hours in a day. Choose carefully what you want to pursue; you don't have to do everything at once. Save some things for later.

7TH MONTH
Aug 8th - Sept 7th 2011

AUSPICIOUS DEVELOPMENTS COME THIS MONTH

The number 8 wealth star pays you a visit, bringing you good fortune luck in abundance. Your efforts earlier in the year start to pay off, and enjoying the results have never felt so satisfying. You enjoy money and wealth luck, some of the windfall variety. With luck like this you can afford to take some risks as long as they are to an extent calculated. To ensure your success can last, keep a positive frame of mind and don't let those who may be jealous of you get into your head. If you let self-doubt creep in you will be your own worst enemy. Your good fortune luck will get magnified if you believe you can achieve what you set out to achieve. Look inwards and not outwards for your strength this month.

WORK & CAREER - *Be Pro-Active*

Money luck is there for the tapping so be sure to carry the **Quick Success talisman** if you are hoping for additional income in the form of commission, a bonus or salary increment in the near future. While your luck is at the top of the cycle, do not waste this time loitering in the background. You may have to be a little more aggressive if you work in a competitive environment. Be pro-active in volunteering yourself to take on more tasks. Show how reliable you are. If you have good ideas, now is the time to share them, as they will more than likely be well received.

BUSINESS - *Stay in Control*
Your wealth luck ripens this month and Sheep people in business will find many opportunities coming their way. You can afford to be bold in your decisions. If you feel in your heart that something is worth pursuing, this is the time to go for it. If you are considering going into business with another party, be sure you stay in the driver's seat. Things will work out well for you nevertheless but you stand to gain more if you are in control. Don't let anyone pull the wool over your eyes or talk you into relinquishing power. A headship position suits you this month, and will be good for the overall partnership as well.

Carry the **Quick Success talisman** to ensure you capture the good luck coming your way this month.

Remember, while you need good co-pilots, you'll do better as the captain of your ship for now.

LOVE & RELATIONSHIPS - *Physical*
The secret to happiness in your relationships this month lies in good communication. Say what you have to say if you want to be truly happy. If you've recently had a misunderstanding, talk about it. Let your feelings out and things between you will be resolved in no time at all. Problems only start if you let any grievances fester. Remember to be able to laugh at yourself. If you are finding it difficult to connect emotionally, sometimes the best way is to go physical. Don't forget the importance of the physical side of relationships.

EDUCATION - *Riding High*
Your ambitions are riding high and you will have a self-assurance that could make somewhat arrogant. Academically this is a good time. Study comes easily and you may well find some of the topics you are covering too easy. The answer is not to make your boredom known to the rest of the class. Keep your egotism to yourself and go with the flow. Just enjoy the fact you are doing well in class.

8TH MONTH
Sept 8th - Oct 7th 2011

CARELESSNESS COULD GET YOU CONNED

This could be a dangerous month with the star of violence entering your chart. There is danger of getting mugged or losing money, so you are advised to be more careful. Avoid taking risks when out and about. Snatch thieves and muggers may strike. Wear or carry some form of **mantra protection** to keep you safe. Do not trust others easily, particularly when it comes to money. Sheep in business risk being taken for a ride. Don't let yourself get careless. New acquaintances that make an appearance in your life this month may not be good news, so watch out. You may have to sustain a small loss; if you do lose some money, consider it the passing of some obstacle or the using up of some bad karma and rejoice. Try and do some charity to counter the misfortune chi arising in your chart.

WORK & CAREER - *Aggravations to Deal With*

You can expect some aggravations at the workplace this month. Just when you are getting comfortable, something could occur to jolt you back to reality. It is important to stay alert this month. Mistakes occur easily, so be more careful. Counter-check your work. Do not leave anything to chance. If you have longtime rivals at work, they may be up to no good again, so to prevent falling victim to office intrigues and the evil eye, carry the **anti-evil-eye amulet** this month. You tend to work better with people of the same gender this month, even if you may not think so. Don't let yourself get involved romantically with anyone from work, as this is likely to explode in a scandal. In extreme circumstances, it could even lead to a dismissal and losing your job.

BUSINESS – Pay Attention to Details

Those of you in business will need to use their shrewdness to stay ahead of the competition, which heats up this month. If you're not on the ball, you could start to lose market share very quickly. There are also dangers of being swindled, so try not to let anything slip by you. Be more vigilant over what is going on in your company. Keep a tight rein on the finances and don't simply enter into deals

The **Anti-Evil Eye Amulet** will help keep you protected against the malicious energies of the month.

without thinking through carefully first. If something does not make sense to you, even if the matter is a small one, make it a point to investigate further. This is a time when paying attention to details will pay off.

LOVE & RELATIONSHIPS – *Rather Complex*

Your love life will have the tendency to become rather complex this month. You may find yourself in the middle of a love triangle or even juggling two lovers. Two-timing can be a dangerous game with severe consequences. Do not cheat on your own partner and do not try to steal someone else's; neither will have good outcomes. Sheep who are married may have to cope with third party interference in their marriage. Make an effort to forge a tighter bond with your spouse, and don't let yourself succumb to outside temptation either. A moment's weakness could have lasting consequences.

EDUCATION – *Stay Focused*

The energies of the month are conducive to quiet study work. Concentrate on doing your own revision rather than depending on friends and tutors. Learn to work on your own. Avoid getting into arguments over things you disagree with others over, as this will only slow you down.

9TH MONTH
Oct 8th - Nov 6th 2011

A HAPPY AND AUSPICIOUS TIME

Things go smoothly for you this month and your relationships with others improve. There is an invisible hand helping you along, and your instincts once again prove spot on. If you're lucky enough to have the benefit of a mentor figure in your life, this month such a person will prove especially helpful in lifting you up to a new level of attainment. This is a good time to embark on new projects and endeavors. Don't waste your favorable luck this month doing nothing. This is not a time to take it easy or to reward yourself with a vacation. Make the most of it because you enjoy superb completion luck right now. To waste it would be a shame.

WORK & CAREER - *Exciting Developments*

There are some exciting developments on the horizon with the potential of upward mobility in your career. Your hard work shows immediate results, and you will be offered more challenging assignments to handle. You will know instinctively if something is going right. You get along well with others this month, so your success is unlikely to lead to envy. Taking on a mentor figure this month will be most beneficial. Having someone who can motivate you to greater heights, or who can help you upwards in your career path will add significantly to the pace at which you get ahead. If you have been thinking of changing jobs and you receive a good alternative offer, you may want to think seriously about it. But be sure not to make any hasty decisions when it comes to your career.

BUSINESS – *Moral Influence*

You can look forward to a productive month ahead when it comes to business. Your staff will look up to you and you hold much moral influence over them at this time. This is a good period to get to know your employees beyond what work they can produce. Learn how they think and what makes them tick if you want your role as boss to be even more effective.

LOVE & RELATIONSHIPS – *Yearning*

You may feel the need to be close to somebody this month. Those of you who are married will find your spouse to be a source of support, comfort and companionship, but if your better half is not providing you all that, you could well get tempted by someone outside of the marriage. The single Sheep will be yearning to settle down with someone; just don't lower your standards just because you're feeling momentarily lonely.

EDUCATION – *A Mentor Helps*
The Young Sheep will benefit tremendously from a mentor figure this month. There may be something on your mind you need advice on. Don't try to make difficult decisions on your own. While you may be feeling all grown-up and feeling prepared to make your own mistakes, there's a less painful way through it, by learning from the experience of those older and wiser than you.

Your parents are probably the best to advise you, but if you feel you need the counsel of somebody else who's not overly close to you, seek out a teacher or a professor. Talking through any dilemmas or anything else on your mind will lift a weight off your chest, but sometimes you need to talk to someone with more experience, rather than just turn to your peers, who may not give you the advice that you need.

10TH MONTH
Nov 7th - Dec 6th 2011

ACCIDENTS OR MISFORTUNE LIKELY

Your chart indicates misfortune and loss, so your luck takes a dip once again. This is a time to be defensive rather than aggressive. The misfortune star in your chart threatens to wreak some havoc in your life, so to escape adversity this month, do try and wear or carry a **five-element pagoda**. This will have the effect of locking up the bad energies that are plaguing the Sheep born this month. Avoid taking risks in work and in business. If you play physical or dangerous sports, be more careful. Elderly Sheep or those suffering from chronic health ailments should definitely avoid staying in a Southwest room this month.

WORK & CAREER - Stay Alert

The workplace is full of crocodiles this month. Although on the surface everyone appears to be your friend, you don't know what is going on behind your back. This is when you need to watch what you say and watch who you share information with. There may be someone trying to politic against you. Adversaries in the workplace are not unique only to you; they will politic against whoever is a suitable target. There is nothing personal about it, so don't get mad or retaliate in a senseless fashion. Stay in control by continuing to do your job well, while removing yourself from the dirty game of corporate backbiting. Develop a certain detachment and look on competition as something to keep you on your toes. You may be under stress and pressure this month, but next month will be better, so stick it out for now.

BUSINESS – *Play Cards Close to Your Chest*

Your luck is afflicted this month, so it is better to lie low. If your systems are working well, stick to the status quo. This is not a good time to introduce new strategies or to make any drastic changes. Focus on your core business and build on what you already have. Avoid taking risks, in particular financial ones. Be wary of going into business with an unknown quantity as you may end up being deceived. There is danger of defamation to your name, so if it is within your control, steer clear of situations that allow others to badmouth you. This is not a good time to make impulsive decisions, so take your time to think things through before deciding. Leave important choices till next month when your luck improves. For now, play your cards close to your chest and don't reveal too much to anyone. You don't know who's on your side and who is not.

LOVE & RELATIONSHIPS - *Luckier Here*

Your love life goes better than your work life this month. You're feeling good when it comes to romance, and your love interest is likely to finally take notice of you. You are well liked by others and receive more attention than usual if you are actively socializing. Avoid blind dates and going along with the whims of friends hoping to play matchmaker. You will have better luck if you stick with your own choice of partner.

EDUCATION - *Somewhat Distracted*

You may find yourself somewhat distracted this month. Small things irk you and you may feel let down by a friend. Don't rely too much on others. You may be emotionally quite fragile, so don't set yourself up for disappointment. In terms of your academic work, do not let small things get in the way of the big picture this month. You know what kind of results you are capable of, so work at staying focused on achieving them rather than battle any self-esteem troubles.

11TH MONTH
Dec 7th - Jan 5th 2012

ALL LOVED IN AND FEELING COZY

This is a month of doubles when the relationship star in your chart gets doubled in strength. This could be good or bad news for you depending on your situation. For those of you in happy family situations, you will be feeling cozy and homely. Some of you will be looking to expand the family, or focused on the kids. If you're still single, you could well have your eye on someone. The main danger is that when the Peach Blossom star gets over-enhanced, for some Sheep, it could lead to infidelity. Protect your marriage by tying an **amethyst geode** to the foot of the bed you share with your spouse. You can also wear the **double happiness symbol** and make your spouse do the same. But most importantly, don't neglect your marriage. Spend quality time together if you value the relationship you have with one another.

Wear the **Double Happiness Symbol** to protect your marriage. This month, risk of external romance threatens.

WORK & CAREER - *Fewer Obstacles*

Your job proceeds with fewer obstacles this month and your relationships with your co-workers also improve. There will be less backbiting and politicking in the workplace this month, making it easier to function and to do your work properly. Make an effort to get to know your colleagues. Think before you speak to ensure you don't inadvertently offend anyone. You don't need unnecessary enemies. You may not share the same ideas with some of your co-workers, but when putting forward your ideas, try and remain as diplomatic as you can. Don't come across intimidating or it may boomerang on you. This month there is some danger of an office romance. Avoid getting involved with someone at work, as there is risk of a sexual scandal that won't do your career any good.

BUSINESS - *New People Bring New Ideas*

Business luck is looking good this month. There are plenty of opportunities coming your way. When something new presents itself, keep an open mind. Investment luck is good over the next few weeks. You may think about broadening your scope of business; as long as you feel right about it, be bold in pursuing new and different things. Mix in different social circles and make an effort to get to know new acquaintances better. Someone you've met recently could bring you just what you've been looking for.

LOVE & RELATIONSHIPS – *Romance Beckons*
Your social calendar fills up quickly in the next few weeks. There are plenty of shared activities for you and your partner, although you'd much rather cozy up at home together. But when duty calls, you always fulfill. Do make time as a couple to have some alone time however. Dinners and soirees are all good but you may be needing some truly quality time just for you and your partner. This may be a good time to go on a second honeymoon of sorts, especially if you haven't done so in a long while. This will do wonders to strengthen your bond with one another, and bring a certain excitement back into your relationship. The single Sheep will also have a busy schedule this month. It is easy to fall for someone you admire from work, but it is best to keep things strictly professional if you value your job.

EDUCATION – *Results*
You have fabulous study luck as the scholastic star is strengthened this month. Avoid rushing your assignments if you want to benefit fully from the favorable stars this month. Put effort into your work and the results will reflect that effort.

12TH MONTH
Jan 6th - Feb 3rd 2012

PATIENCE IS A BENEFICIAL VIRTUE

The quarrelsome star brings misunderstandings into your life and makes you more quick-tempered than usual. While the Sheep person is usually quite mild-mannered and tolerant, this month friends could find you're not yourself at all, snapping at every little thing. Learn to be more patient with others if you want them to extend the same courtesy towards you. Callous remarks could hurt someone dear to you, and could cause a chain of events that you will live to deeply regret. Be careful also when it comes to dealing with the authorities. Committing a minor offence like getting a parking ticket could give you far more hassle than you bargained for.

WORK & CAREER - *Some Challenges to Face*

There are challenges to face at the workplace this month. Keep a grip on your temper or you may end up making enemies you don't need. Working alone will serve you better than trying to integrate into a team right now. You get along with others fine, until you disagree on something, and then you find it hard to let go. Try not to be overly stubborn because others won't take kindly to that kind of attitude. You can stand firm, but not at all costs. This month it is better to lie low than to take too high a profile. Put in effort to do your work well, but don't attempt to be the superstar everyone has to take notice of; you could fall flat on your face.

BUSINESS - *Take a Break*
The energies of the month do little to help you, so you're pretty much left to fend for yourself. You're more irritable than usual, so making a good impression at meetings, especially when the discussion gets heated, may not be something you're so good at right this moment. If you have important negotiations to get through, it is probably wiser to send your best general than to take on the task yourself. This is a good time to take a break, relax, go on holiday. Business will carry on fine without you, and being relaxed will make you more amicable, more likeable and easier to do business with.

LOVE & RELATIONSHIPS - *Prickly*
The closer you are to your partner, the greater the chances you'll get on each other's nerves this month. It may help you to get some things off your chest, but always recognize when to draw the line. If you

cannot have a civil discussion, it is a good idea to have some time alone. Time apart from each other could actually draw you closer, so taking a short break could be the best solution for now. Another way to improve relations between the two of you is to plan on doing something enjoyable together.

HOME & FAMILY – *Mix with Others*

There are some angry stars plaguing you this month, and your temper is just as bad in the home as it is at the workplace. A change of routine may give your spirits the lift it needs. Get in touch with old friends you haven't seen in a while, or arrange a meal with some new acquaintances. Mixing with people you don't know so well will help steer your disposition in the right direction.

EDUCATION – *Frustrating*

It could be a frustrating time for the student Sheep because you feel you are being pulled in so many different directions. The stars in your char this month also make you more impatient and quick-tempered than usual. Take a deep breath and relax. Don't let others pressure you to a point where it is difficult to perform. And trust those who have your best interests at heart.

Important Feng Shui Updates for 2011

Part 6

If you have been following the advice given in these Fortune & Feng Shui books on annual feng shui updates, you are already familiar with the time dimension of feng shui which protects against negative luck each year.

This requires overall cleansing and re-energizing of the energy of the home to prepare for the coming of a new year, while simultaneously making placement changes to accommodate a new pattern of chi distribution. Getting rid of old items and replacing with specially made new remedial cures that are in tune with the year's chi brings pristine and fresh new luck into the home.

It is vital to anticipate and quickly suppress the source of malicious chi brought by the new feng shui winds of the year, as this ensures that bad chi originating in afflicted sectors never have a chance to gather, accumulate, grow strong and then ripen in a burst of bad luck! With powerful remedies in place, this will not happen, thereby keeping residents safe from misfortune that can be unsettling and heartbreaking.

Severe bad luck that brings despair can happen to anyone. Sometimes, even in the midst of some personal triumphant moment, your world can suddenly crumble before you. Last year for instance, the world witnessed the incredibly sad falling apart of the marriages of **Kate Winslet** and **Sandra Bullock** soon after they each had reached the pinnacle of their profession by winning the Oscar for Best Actress. Kate had won in 2009 and Sandra in 2010.

Both had gushed and thanked their husbands in their acceptance speeches, obviously unaware of destructive energies lurking within their homes. Both husbands - for whatever reasons - were looking for satisfaction elsewhere outside their marriages! Kate's husband, noted director Sam Mendes' eyes had already started roving in 2009... but the marriage had fallen apart only in 2010 when the grief-bringing star of infidelity made its appearance. Both actresses do not believe in luck... and it is safe to assume they are too busy to have the time to pause, and arrange for the placement of feng shui cures in their homes.

Those not following time dimension feng shui from these books are unlikely to have known that last year 2010 was a year when the external romance star of peach blossom was lurking in every household, creating the potential to cause havoc in marriages! It was vital last year to place cures in the home to protect against outsider third party interference. Sandra Bullock and Kate Winslet are just two of the high profile victims of the star of *External Peach Blossom*! They are exquisitely beautiful ladies, but both of their marriages unraveled in March of 2010!

It is therefore so important that each time we cross into a new year, we should note the particular ailments and afflictions of the year, and then carefully bring in the antidotes so we can sail through the year without having to endure the consequences of bad feng shui, which of course can manifest in different ways. No matter how it manifests, bad luck always brings distress, heartbreak and a sense of helplessness. Why go through this kind of unhappiness when you can prevent or reduce it?

Each year there will be the same kinds of afflictions bringing illness, accidents, robbery, quarrels and misfortune, but these afflictions change location each year and vary in strength from year to year. So we need to systematically suppress these *"staples of bad luck"* first.

Then there are the disturbing stars of misfortune - these too need to be neutralized mainly with element therapy so that they do not cast their ill influence onto your luck. In some years, there can be some hazardous or dangerous alignment of energies we need to be careful of, and these also need to be addressed. For instance, we have already told you about the four pillars of clashing elements bringing severe quarrelsome energy that can get violent.

It is SO vital for everyone to be alert to dangers in the bigger picture. This is a year when concerted efforts must be made to protect yourself and your family; safeguard your house energy and everyone in it from getting hit by the conflicting elements of the year.

Using Incense
To overcome the year's overriding disharmonious energies, an effective way is to use incense as a way of dispelling bad energy.

Incense is a powerful way of transcending time and space blending heaven and earth energies to chase away afflictions that bring disaster, setbacks and accidents. In fact, incense (and scents) although invisible, are a powerful way of overcoming obstacles and they have been used by all the major traditions of the world.

Incense is one of the more powerful methods used to overcome obstacles that block your luck. If you find that you keep missing opportunities, or that deals already brokered, sealed and agreed upon keep getting spoiled or cancelled, then you need to use incense.

This is part of spiritual feng shui cleansing - this is the third dimension of inner feng shui that can make a real difference to clearing the way for good fortune to flow unimpeded into your life.

This is because creating a regular infusion of incense (with some smoke) works incredibly well for clearing the pathway for good chi energy to flow into your home; and with empowering symbolic placements, these can work together to create the lucky ambience you need. Home energy then becomes harmonious and benevolent, blending beautifully with new patterns of chi formations that are flowing through your home. Just try infusing your space with the special blend of sandalwood or pine incense and feel the difference instantly!

Focusing on your house feng shui from this perspective will help you enjoy a better year, irrespective of how good or how bad the indications for the year may be. This is because a regular use of incense can go a long way to subduing the afflictions in corners of the house that affect your animal sign, hence protecting you from the affliction of that corner. Incense also helps strengthen the placement cures that suppress feng shui time afflictions.

Misfortunes are always worse and have nastier consequences when they catch you unaware. You may feel that you simply cannot cope when faced with the prospect of losing your job, your home, your good name, your child, your lover or your spouse. But these can all be avoided when afflictive energies are effectively suppressed. Then also whatever bad event may occur becomes more manageable. Sometimes when the cures are strong, they can even be avoided. This is the wonderful promise and benefit of creating good timely feng shui in the home. And when divine assistance is invoked through the wearing of powerful amulets and sacred talismans the remedies become even more powerful. This brings harmony and smooth sailing through the year.

Luck is never static

Luck occurs in cycles and the key to continuing good fortune is to know when the luck of your home is at its peak and when it requires extra protection. When important areas of the house gets hit by misfortune-bringing stars, everyone living within gets hurt. In the same way when these same areas are visited by lucky stars, everyone in the house enjoys good luck.

To what degree this incidence of good and bad luck affects residents depends also on their personal outlook for the year. Cycles of luck affect different people in different ways and this is one reason why it can be so beneficial to analyze how the year affects your animal sign. Here we are not just talking about 12 animal signs.

Consider the **infinite variations** of each individual's pattern of luck when you factor in the two sets of elements in the four sets of birth data - **Year, Month, Day & Hour** of Birth... then factor in the house, the locations of the main door, the bedroom, the dining and living area...

Factor in also the **changing energies** of the year as well as the energy of the people who surround you, make up your circle of family and friends ... and you will be awed by the mathematical combinations of chi that are affecting you **every single moment!**

We cannot take care of everything that affects our luck, but we sure can take care of enough to ensure a pretty good and smooth year. And once we are assured that we have been adequately protected, we can then turn our attention to maximizing good fortune for the year... Success, Love, Satisfaction with Life, Money, Wealth, Career highs, Contentment... and a lot more can then be induced to manifest into our lives. This depends on what we want, what we energize for and how we enhance our bedrooms, work spaces and living areas. It is really easier than you think! Just protect against bad luck and energize for good luck.

You must first protect your **main door** and your **bedroom**. Where these two vital spots of your house are located must be protected against bad numbers or bad stars. Afflictive energy can be illness or misfortune numbers, hostile or robbery stars. These can, together with other kinds of negative energy, cause loss of some kind. Someone could force you into litigation - this is something that will happen more often than normal this year; you might suffer perhaps a break up of an important relationship - this too is unfortunately being fanned by the destructive patterns of elements this year.

Severe bad luck or loss when it manifests, is always traumatic. Feng shui corrections offer the solutions to avoiding or at least diminishing the chances of negativities happening. Knowing feng shui enables you to anticipate a potentially problematic year; and then to do something about it.

Correcting and suppressing bad energy is rarely difficult. But it requires a bit of effort.

What you need to do is to systematically go through each of the nine sectors of your home - mentally dividing your home into a three-by-three sector grid that corresponds to eight compass directions with a center. The next step is to study the year's charts; first the Annual Feng Shui chart which pinpoints the afflicted parts of the home, then the 24 mountain charts which show the "*stars*", both lucky and unlucky, that also influence the year's distribution of luck, and finally, the year's four pillars chart. It is the collective and unified analysis of these indications that point to what needs to be done to safeguard the feng shui of any abode.

Suppressing Flying Star Afflictions for the Year

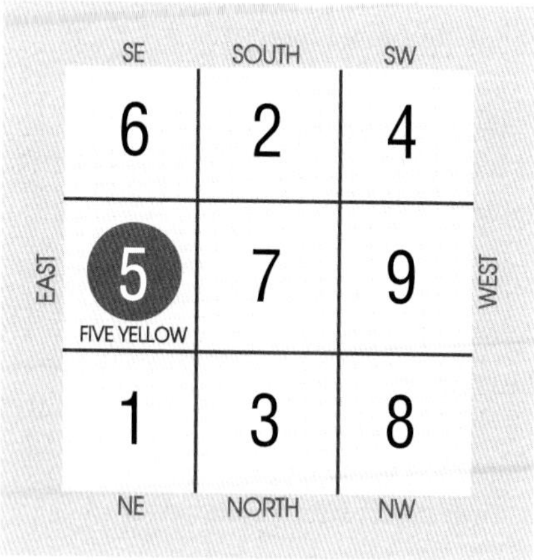

SE	SOUTH	SW
6	2	4
5 FIVE YELLOW	7	9
1	3	8
NE	NORTH	NW

EAST (left side), WEST (right side)

Traditionally, one of the more important things to update prior to each new year is to find the new locations for all the afflictive star numbers and then to deal with each of them. These yearly afflictions are the same each year, but their strength and severity vary from year to year, depending on where they are. The element of each affliction interacts with the element of the sector they fly into. In some years for instance, the misfortune star number of five yellow a.k.a. **wu wang** can be really strong while in some years they are weaker.

In 2011, the *wu wang* flies to the East, where its Earth element is strongly suppressed by the Wood element here. The 2011 *wu wang* is thus not as strong as it was in the previous year when it occupied the Southwest. There the Earth element of the Southwest strengthened the *wu wang*.

In 2011 therefore, we are not so afraid of this otherwise feared star. In spite of this, it is still advisable to keep it under control in case someone in the house is going through weak Life Force year or whose Spirit Essence may be lacking. The East is the home location of the Rabbit, so the *wu wang* hurts the Rabbit more than anyone else.

Remedies against the Wu Wang

In spite of this, do place traditional remedies to suppress *wu wang* in the East. The *wu wang* is a thoroughly unpleasant star number whose effect could suddenly manifest if your bedroom happens to be here affected by it and it is also being hit by some secret unknown poison arrow, which can act as a catalyst for the wu wang to erupt; or when the Wood element here gets inadvertently weakened for whatever reason.

The *wu wang* blocks success and affects the luck of the eldest son of the family. So to be safe, get the cures that have been specially designed for the year and place these in the East sectors.

Do not forget the East walls of your important rooms and also the living and family areas where you and your family spend a great deal of time. Place the cures on a sideboard or table, not on the floor!

Five Element Pagoda with Tree of Life

In 2011, we are recommending the five element pagoda that comes with a wood base and is decorated with an all-powerful Tree of Life that grows from the base of the pagoda right to the tip. There are three pairs of birds on the branches of the tree of

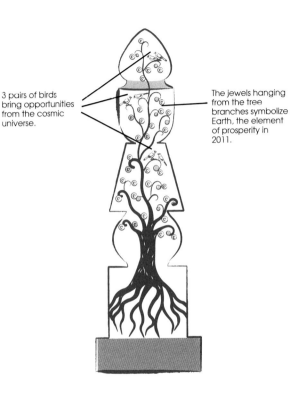

3 pairs of birds bring opportunities from the cosmic universe.

The jewels hanging from the tree branches symbolize Earth, the element of prosperity in 2011.

The **five element pagoda** with Tree of Life transforms the *wu wang* into a wealth-bringing star.

life. These birds bring opportunities from the cosmic constellations and legend has it they attract exactly the kind of luck a household needs. From the leaves of the tree hang glittering jewels which signify the treasures of the earth, the element that symbolizes wealth and prosperity in 2011. This powerful five element pagoda is actually a transforming tool which turns the all-powerful *wu wang* into a wealth-enhancing tool. Note that this powerful pagoda synchronizes extremely well with the energies of 2011 and 2012 when the *wu wang* flies to the Wood sectors of the compass. It is usually not used during other years.

Metal Bell with Tree of Life

Another very beneficial cure for the 2011 *wu wang* is the powerful Bell which is also made of metal but has a wooden mallet, so the sound created is more mellow and lower than that of an all-metal bell. The handle of the bell is made of wood; and on the bell itself there is again the amazing tree of life to strengthen the Wood chi of the East; and the tree also has 6 birds on its branches; and with jewels on its leaves to signify wealth luck.

The **Metal Bell with wooden handle** is another enhancing tool that simultaneously suppresses the *wu wang*.

This transforms the five element bell into an empowering tool which, even as it suppresses the *wu wang*, is simultaneously sending out powerful vibrations each time the sounds of the bell are created. This way, the bell utilizes the *wu wang* to attract great good fortune opportunities and it is by placing a tree of life with 6 birds that gives it these attributes. We have also embossed the *dependent arising mantra* onto both the **five element bell** and **pagoda**.

This powerful mantra greatly empowers these cures! Those wanting to wear these powerful symbols over the two years 2011 and 2012 can consider wearing either the pagoda or the bell with the tree design to safeguard themselves from the wu wang.

The Sheep born must be watchful in February as well as November, when the *wu wang* flies into your month chart. For you, the *wu wang* brings discord and temporary problems into your marital relationship. It is worthwhile to place the cures in your home location of Southwest, because here, the *wu wang* is very strong.

Misfortunes caused by the *wu wang* in 2011 are not as severe as in other years, but are nonetheless annoying and aggravating. It can cause problems with employees or act as a catalyst for other kinds of bad luck to erupt, so it is a good idea to suppress its negative effect. This year's cure does just that, but it also uses the inherent strength of the *wu wang* to transform bad luck into something good.

If you reside in a room located in the East of your house, place the pagoda inside your bedroom. Make sure it is in place before February 3rd which is the start of the lunar new year 2011. It is also important to take note that there should not be any renovations done in the East side of the house through 2011.

Avoid all kinds of demolition or digging work although there are some feng shui masters who say that building works are not harmful, arguing that anything productive will not harm the household. We disagree as the wu wang should not be activated by any kind of building. This only strengthens it.

Planting a tree in the East is however very auspicious, especially if you do this on **February 4th**, the day of the **lap chun**!

Other Afflictions of the 2011 Chart

SE	SOUTH	SW
6	2 ILLNESS STAR	4
EAST 5	7	9 WEST
1	3	8
NE	NORTH	NW

The illness causing star flies to the South in 2011.
This is an Earth element star flying into a Fire sector, so here, the illness star gets considerably strengthened, making it a serious threat to residents, but especially for anyone residing in the South sector of the house; but the illness star affects everyone if it is where the main door into the house is located.

Any house that faces or sits South will find that residents within are more vulnerable to catching viruses and falling ill more easily. Try using another door to enter and leave the house by, to avoid overactivating the South.

Should the main door of the house be in the South, the constant opening and closing of the door will energize the star, making it more likely to bring illness into the house and this is pronounced during the months of **March** and **December** when the month stars mirror that of the year hence bringing a double whammy to afflicted sectors.

If your door is facing South, it is a good idea to use another door located in another sector (if possible) especially during these two months.

If this is not possible then it is necessary to exhaust the Earth element of the illness star placing something metallic or made of wood here.

It is necessary also to remove all Earth element items such as crystals, porcelain vases or stone objects from the South. Also keep lights in the South dim to reduce Fire element energy.

Cures for the Illness Star of 2011

Over the years, we have found that the best way to suppress illness energy brought by the intangible flying star 2 is to suppress its negative effect with a wu lou shaped container made of metal - either in brass or steel. To the Chinese, the wu lou is a container for keeping herbal cures, so that over the years it has come to signify medicinal qualities. Many of China's favorite deities and especially the **Goddess of Mercy, Kuan Yin** are usually depicted carrying a small wu lou shaped little bottle that is said to contain healing nectar.

Placing a large **wu lou** in the South generates invisible healing energies for both physical as well as mental afflictions. It is as good as medicine, and in fact, it is also a very good idea to place a small wu lou by your bedside so that it exudes healing energies even as you sleep. This is good feng shui!

You can also invoke the help of the powerful healing Buddha, also known as the **Medicine Buddha**. This is the blue-bodied Buddha whose image and mantra create so many blessings that the residents of any home that displays the Medicine Buddha image in any way at all, especially in the sector where the illness flying star is located, ill enjoy good health, rarely if ever falling sick. It is a good idea in 2011 to have an image of **Medicine Buddha** placed on a table top in the **North** part of any room where you spend a great deal of time.

Those feeling poorly in 2011 should also wear **Medicine Buddha bracelets** or our specially designed **moving mantra watches** - the only watches of its kind in the world! We brought out the first such moving mantra watch last year and they have since helped so many people that we have extended our range to include a watch with the healing image of the Medicine Buddha. Wearing such a watch is like having prayers being constantly recited for your good health. It is truly amazing how far technology has progressed. To us, it makes sense to utilize all the technical advances that have made so many wonderful new products possible. Many of the advances in technology have made feng shui very easy to practice.

Wearing the Medicine Buddha pendant will help those feeling poorly this year.

The Quarrelsome Hostile Star flies to the North in 2011

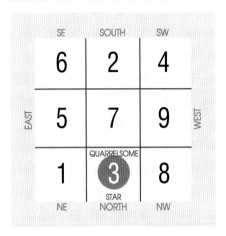

This is a Wood element star flying into a Water element sector. As such, this noisy, litigation-bringing star number is both strong and harder to overcome. It is dangerous and aggravating and very capable of causing anyone staying in the North sector a great deal of problems. This is the major affliction affecting anyone having a bedroom in the North sector in 2011.

You are likely to be more easily stressed out and this will affect your productivity levels. For some, it can even create obstacles that block your luck. At its worst, the effect of this affliction is to be hit with someone bringing you into litigation, causing you no end of aggravating pressure and inconveniences, or someone getting violent with you. This star brings a pervasive feeling of hostility, short tolerance levels and a great deal of impatience. There will be arguments, fights and misunderstandings for everyone directly hit by it.

Unfortunately for anyone having a bedroom in the **North** sector of the house, the **quarrelsome star 3 is made stronger** this year because its Wood Element is produced even more by the Water element of the North.

As a Wood element star, the best way to subdue its effect is to exhaust it with Fire Element energy. Anything that suggests Fire is an excellent cure, so bright lights and the color red are excellent remedies. Hence, because the North is associated with water energy, the danger is enhanced so remedying it is vital.

Carry the **Red Dragon Amulet** to subdue quarrelsome energies through the year.

If you are afflicted by this star make sure you are not hurt by it in any way by carrying the **Red Dragon amulet**. This brings luck while keeping the 3 star subdued. Note that this amulet has the Dragon carrying a sword in its right claw as this helps overcome all the clashing elements of the year.

The Violent Star 7 attracts bad people into the home

The Violent Star 7 which attracts bad people into the home is in the center of the chart this year, where it is symbolically locked up, hence reducing its influence. This is an affliction which hurts most when it occupies one of the outer sectors of any building, but trapped in the center, its negative impact is less severe. The number 7 star number is an Metal element number and with the center being an Earth sector, here we have a situation of Earth producing Metal, so while it may be hemmed in in the center, it is nevertheless troublesome. It is a number that causes loss through being cheated or robbed.

A good way of keeping this affliction under wraps is simply to place a small sideboard in the center of the house, place seven pieces of metal within and then lock it up. This symbolically "*locks up*" the number 7 star very effectively. At the same time, have **a Blue Rhino with a 6-tusk Elephant** near the entrance into the home.

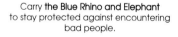

Carry **the Blue Rhino and Elephant** to stay protected against encountering bad people.

However, should any of you be feeling vulnerable with the burglary star in the center of the home, you can safeguard yourself by carrying the **Blue Rhino & Elephant** or using it as a hanging on your bags or hung in the car. It is good practice to stay protected against encountering bad people who would want to harm you. Use the **Blue Rhino & Elephant protector** as this continues to be an effective cure in 2011. It is a highly respected cure against the potential violence of the 7.

Note that the problem with the number 7 star in 2011 is that being in the center of the feng shui chart, the number 7 can potentially spread its influence into any part of the house, hence it is necessary to keep it well under control.

The best is to literally "*lock it up*", otherwise it simply plays havoc with house security. It is very inconvenient and even dangerous when the 7 star number strikes.

In 2011
the God of the Year cannot be ignored

The Tai Sui is important because this year it directly faces the *Star of Natural Disaster* in the West. This is a 24 mountain star that sits between the two stars of *three killings*! That there are such intensive negative stars directly confronting the Tai Sui is not good for the year. It suggests a battle, and when a battle takes place, there is always collateral damage! Especially when they are read against the background of the year's clashing elements in the four pillars; these signs collectively indicate clear and present danger.

How the dangers of the year manifest will vary in timing and severity for different houses and different countries; but generally, an afflicted Tai Sui means that the wars of the world currently being waged on several fronts are unlikely to decline. There is also no let up in the occurrence of natural disasters.

Do be extra mindful of the Tai Sui in 2011. Avoid confronting it. Avoid facing East and make extra efforts not to "*disturb*" its location, the East sector of the house. This sector must be kept quiet as noise activates the Tai Sui and incurs its wrath. Also avoid digging, banging or renovating this side of the home.

It is beneficial to place a well-executed art piece of the beautiful Pi Yao in the East as this celestial creature is excellent for appeasing the Tai Sui. The Pi Yao always brings good feng shui and it is for this reason that you will find many artistic variations of this auspicious creature all over China and Hong Kong. It is a great favorite with people who believe in feng shui. It brings exceptional good fortune into the home.

For 2011, a Pi Yao made in Earth element material is preferred, as this element signifies wealth luck. So crystal or ceramic Pi Yao, or one made in liu li medium, would be excellent.

Place a **Pi Yao** in the East sector of the home this year to appease the Tai Sui who resides here in 2011.

It is important for everyone whose bedroom is in the **East,** or whose sitting direction while working is facing or sitting East, to place the **Pi Yao** near you.

It does not matter if the Pi Yao is standing or sitting but it should appear proud and majestic looking. The more beautiful looking the Pi Yao is, the better it is to display in the house to appease the Tai Sui. This advice applies to anyone irrespective of their animal sign. The place of the Tai Sui is taken very seriously in feng shui. It is emphasized in the *Treatise on Harmonizing Times and Distinguishing Directions* compiled under the patronage of the Qianlong Emperor during his reign in the mid-Eighteenth century and any Master practicing feng shui in China or Hong Kong always ensures the Tai Sui is respected and thus taken account of in their updating process.

The Emperor Qiang Lung inspired Treatise states that the locations where the Tai Sui resides and where the Tai Sui has just vacated are lucky locations. So note that in 2011, the locations of East and NE1 are considered lucky benefiting from the lingering energy of the Tai Sui. Those having their rooms in these two locations will enjoy the patronage and protection of the Tai Sui in 2011. The Treatise further explains that it is unlucky to reside in the location where the Tai Sui is progressing towards i.e. clockwise on the astrology compass. In 2011 this means the Southeast 1 location; it is unlucky to directly confront the Tai Sui's residence. It is unlucky to "*face*" the Tai Sui because this is deemed rude, so the advice for 2011 is to not to directly face East.

In 2011, never forget to avoid confronting the Tai Sui. **Do not face East this year** even if this is your success direction under the Kua formula of personalized lucky directions.

Carry the **Tai Sui Amulet** to subdue the Grand Duke Jupiter.

Those who forget and inadvertently face the Tai Sui run the risk of offending the Tai Sui. This brings obstacles to your work life. Your road to achieving success gets constantly interrupted and for some, supporters can turn into adversaries.

In 2011, the West of every building is afflicted by the Three Killings

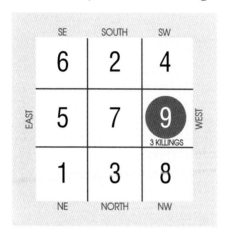

This affliction brings three severe misfortunes associated with loss, grief and sadness. Its location each year is charted according to the animal sign that rules the year. Thus in 2011 it flies to the West because the Rabbit belongs to the Triangle of Affinity made up of the Rabbit, Sheep and Boar; with the Rabbit occupying a cardinal direction (East).

The Three Killings is thus in the West, the direction that is directly opposite the Rabbit. This feng shui aggravation affects only primary directions, so unlike other feng shui afflictions, the direct bad effects of the *three killings* are felt over a larger area of the house. When you suffer a sudden reversal of fortune, it is usually due to being hit by the three killings.

In 2011 the *three killings* resides in the West, where it poses some danger to the young daughters of the family. Anyone occupying the West would be vulnerable to being hit by the *three killings*. For everyone whose bedroom and/or main doors face West or are located in the West sector of your home, please get the celestial protectors - the Chi Lin, the Fu Dog and the Pi Yao - preferably made colorful and with a fierce expression. Place them close together, either on a coffeetable or sideboard; get them in brass and enamel. For them to be effective, some texts refer also to the three different deities traditionally seated on their backs, but as a feng shui cure, they are as effective on their own or with the Deities, although the secret is to make certain they have their different implements with them as these enable them to symbolically overcome the afflictions.

The **Sword** on the back of the **Pi Yao** protects against loss of wealth. The **Lasso** on the back of the **Chi Lin** to protects against loss of loved one. The **Steel Hook** on the back of the **Fu Dog** protects against loss of good name. The hook is a very powerful implement which also *"hooks in wealth luck"*.

These 3 celestial guardians are extremely effective; but this year an old Taoist master has advised to also add in the implements, and confirmed that as feng shui cures, they work best when new. This ensures that their energy is strong. Do not use antique images as feng shui cures as these are usually surrounded by tired chi. It is important that feng shui remedies have fresh energy so there is strong vigor and vitality chi attached to them. Antique furniture decorated with celestials can be lovely to look at, but they rarely make powerful cures. They can however generate auspicious chi after they are cleansed of lingering yin vibes.

Use a dry cloth with either sea salt or crystal salt to wipe off stale chi and they should be fine. Do this cleansing ritual at least once a year. The month before the lunar new year is a good time. The energy of the *three killings* can sometimes stick onto furniture, especially those that have animals or human images painted onto them. It is a good idea to use raw salt as a way of wiping off lingering bad chi. Those of who may want to stay protected from the *three killings* and prevent them from overwhelming you when you are out and about this year can also hang the **three celestials amulet** on your handbags and pocket books. Those of you staying in the West sectors of the house, you could experience bad dreams and nightmares and if so, make sure you place the **three celestial guardians** on a cabinet along the West wall of the room. If you have a window in the bedroom, place the three celestials there even if it is not the West wall. The presence of the three guardians is a powerful cosmic force that protects.

Display the **3 celestial protectors** in the West to counter the 3 Killings affliction in 2011. It is even better when these protectors carry the implements of the Deities they are associated with, as these enable them to effectively overcome the afflictions.

Strengthening the Right
& Countering the Left of Sheep's Luck

The Sheep enjoys the *Star of Big Auspicious* brought to its right by the stars of the 24 mountains in 2011. This is very auspicious as it is coming from the direction of the Horse, its very special soulmate and secret friend. This star should be activated by shining a bright light in the location of its residence in 2011, which is the South 3 sector.

On the Sheep's left is the *Star of Yin House* and this tends to bring unsettling energy to the Sheep's space. The yin house must be countered by the presence of lights and sounds here in the direction SW2. By bringing bright lights into the vicinity of the Sheep's location will pull in big dose of good fortune luck for the Sheep in 2011.

THE 24 MOUNTAIN STARS CHART OF 2011

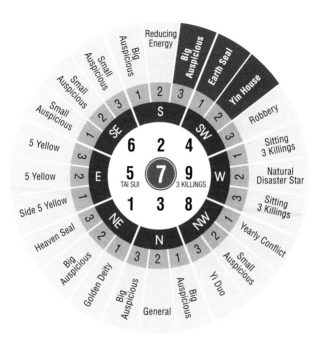

The Sheeps SW1 location is flanked by Big Auspicious
and Yin House in 2011.

Suppressing Anger Vibrations

We have already noted that the North is the sector where the angry star 3 has flown to in 2011. This can be suppressed by using the **Red Dragon Amulet**. Anger vibrations are usually the cause of many problems, so those residing in the North corners of their home should subdue this affliction.

Another two excellent ways to prevent anger vibrations getting out of hand involve the use of incense. This is because scents, aromas, incense are powerful mediums that can transcend the cosmic fields of energy that bring negative energy to us. We have spent the past year talking about the third dimension of feng shui and the use of aromatic incense is one of the more common ways used by Masters skilled in the shamanistic aspects of feng shui practice. At its most basic, joss sticks for instance are used during the Wealth God welcoming rituals performed during the night before the lunar new year; during such rituals very pungent and strong smells such as sandalwood are used.

Incense can be used through the year. They can be used to clear the air of negatives; to suppress troublesome energies that bring aggravations that disturb the mind thereby leading to bad temper.

Incense is associated with the transcendence of chi energy between cosmic realms of consciousness, and are an advanced form of energy practice used in the old days by expert practitioners. They are powerful yet invisible instruments for dissolving concentrations of negative energy. The number 3 star is one example of a concentration of energy that brings aggravations. It is good feng shui to dissolve its effect.

Another excellent way to stay immune to the 3 star is to utilize calming aromas, and in the case of anyone staying in the North, you can use incense for the outdoors, and for your bedroom, you can try using lavender aroma which is relaxing and soothing when infused into the atmosphere.

But if anger vibrations are too strong, then incense rituals must be used and this can be done outdoors. Then anger vibrations will be very effectively suppressed. Incense also appease spiritual landlords in the area and they will help to dissolve all negativities that cause hostile energy to burst into big quarrels. Burn sandalwood or pine incense regularly in the North in 2011.

Activating the Trinity of Tien Ti Ren

In the year 2011, **all four primary directional locations** - North, South, East and West - are afflicted, as we have seen with the *Illness*, *Hostile*, *Five Yellow* and *Natural Disaster* star. Of the four, only the West location has the lucky 9 star number, but 9 in a Metal element sector always contains hidden dangers; so correcting and placing remedies to safeguard the cardinal locations of the house is extremely important in 2011.

The **four secondary directions** on the other hand, are indicating extremely lucky star numbers, with 8 leading the way as it flies into the patriarchal corner of Northwest, followed by the heavenly 6 in the opposite direction of Southeast. Then there is the *Victory Star* in the Northeast and the star of romance and scholarship in the Southwest in 2011.

With this kind of star number configurations, we also note that the Northeast/Southwest axis (which is the favorable axis of this current period of 8) has been blessed with the star of earth seal in the SW and the matching counterpart star of the *Heaven Seal* in the Northeast. The presence of these heaven and earth stars are indicative of the need for the trinity of lucky cosmic forces to be present in the North and the South, the other set of axis direction which are showing a set of two *Big Auspicious* stars. In N1 and N3 and also in S1 and S3, we see here a quartet of important lucky stars brought by the circle of the 24 mountains.

In 2011, there is the strong indication of substantial changes taking place in the world which will **bring benefits to some** and **loss to others**. This is vital to understand, as the year itself is showing a set of four pillars which not only has **4 sets of clashing elements** but also **two yang and two yin pillars**. This suggests that the complementarily of cosmic forces is balanced. **Yin and yang are in balance**.

Good fortune manifests as growth, sudden windfalls and big transformations of luck that bring a "*house filled with jewels*" enabling one to "*wear the jade belt*" if the household successfully activates the trinity of *Tien Ti Ren*. In other words, there must be plentiful supply of heaven, earth and mankind energies! This is something that is beneficial to ensure at all times, but more so in 2011, where severe bad luck indications are balanced against equally powerful auspicious indications. So the important thing is to tap into the positive energies of the year, thereby getting onto the growth spiral. *Tien ti ren* is the key! Symbolically, just placing the words heaven and earth is often good enough to complement the presence of people within a home.

Mankind chi is the powerful *yang* chi that activates the *yin* earth chi and the cosmic heaven chi.

In the old days, wealthy households would always include miniature mountains to signify Earth, and also all the Deities of their faith Taoism or Buddhism, the **8 Immortals** and the **18 Holy Beings** - all to signify heaven chi while at the same time imbuing their homes with activity and celebrations to signify mankind chi. This infusion of yang energy acts a catalyst to generate the presence of the powerful cosmic trinity.

In this way did wealthy households of the past live, and over the years, these practices came to signify the cultural underpinnings of the Chinese way of life. Thus one should not be surprised to note that many Chinese households believe that the blessing power of heaven is brought in by the presence of deities on their family altar. The family altar was always placed rather grandly, directly facing the front door. This signified the continuing presence of heaven luck. It was important to keep the family altars clean with offerings of food, lights, water, wine and incense made daily.

Wealthier households would even have professionals such as monks and holy men, who would come and recite prayers for the family at special dates in the year. These were daily rituals believed to keep the family patriarch safe and the household in a state of abundance. In other words, keeping their lifestyles secure.

In addition, good Earth chi was assured by the presence of mountains and rivers simulated in landscaped gardens around the family home and symbolized by **mountain scenery paintings** inside the home. Good feng shui also ensures good chi flows in abundance through the rooms and corridors of the house.

Finally, excellent mankind chi is kept flowing fresh and revitalizing yang energy. **Auspicious phrases** and lucky rhyming couplets were placed as **artistic calligraphy** in important rooms of the house; this was the equivalent of today's very popular "*affirmation*s".

The Chinese have been living with these powerful affirmations for as long as anyone can remember, and there are literally thousands of such lucky phrases such as "*your wealth has arrived*" or "your luck is as long as the yellow river"... and so forth. These are popular sayings exchanged between families during festive seasons and during Chinese New Year. Anyone wanting to enjoy good fortune continuously must be mindful of the power generated by *tien ti ren* chi inside their homes. This is very timely for 2011 to help you benefit from the year.

In 2011 therefore, the three dimensions of feng shui space and time as well as the dimension which engages the cosmic force within the self (the purest source of yang energy generated from within you) must all be present. In fact, this is a major secret of feng shui. This is the mankind chi that pulls heaven and earth chi together. Good mankind chi requires you to stay positive, to generate lucky aspirations and to anticipate good outcomes. Your expectations must be high. You can enhance the empowerment of your own self. This unlocks for you the strength of mankind luck - *ren* chi - which pulls time and space into a powerful whole. With this kind of attitude, you can then start to enhance the four lucky secondary directions with powerful enhancing placement feng shui:

Enhancing the Chi of 8 in the Northwest

The all-powerful and auspicious 8 flies to the place of the patriarch in 2011, bringing quite exceptional great good fortune to all the father figures of the world.

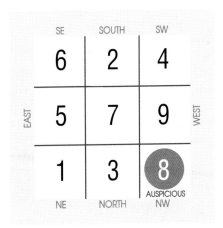

Being located in the Northwest, the 8 Earth Star also gets very considerably strengthened, especially since it is flying to the NW from the center where it was located last year.

As an annual star number, the 8 is indeed very strong. It brings good relationship luck and it brings success and wealth. It is a powerful star at its zenith.

What worked last year, the **crystal 8** embedded with real 24 carat gold, continues to work this year, so do display it in the Northwest of the house; or of your office. But the crystal 8 becomes even more powerful when it is placed alongside a **crystal Ru Yi**, the **scepter of authority**. This is especially beneficial for Chief Executive Officers i.e. CEOs and bosses; in fact, anyone in a position of authority and power will benefit from the Ru Yi placed alongside the 8.

In the old days, these symbols were recommended for mandarins at court - equivalent to the Ministers and top business leaders of today. Those who want a boost to their career should consider placing this powerful symbol of advancement and upward mobility in the Northwest corner of their home, office or home office.

With the 8 flying into the Northwest, the Ru Yi placed next to the 8 becomes especially effective. Place the Ru Yi in exactly the middle of the NW sector i.e. in NW2, as this is the auspicious part of this location.

Place a **Ru YI** alongside a **crystal 8** for career strength and longevity.

Activating
the Power of Heavenly 6 in the Southeast

The number 6, a lucky white star usually associated with the cosmic energies of heaven, flies to the Southeast in 2011, directly facing the Northwest, thereby creating a powerful alliance between heaven and earth luck, bringing luck not only to the Southeast but also to the Northwest, directly opposite.

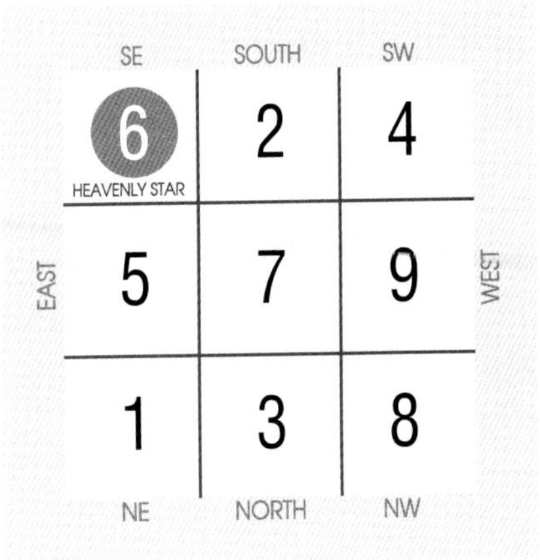

SE	SOUTH	SW
6 HEAVENLY STAR	2	4
5	7	9
1	3	8
NE	NORTH	NW

(EAST on left side, WEST on right side)

There is great synergy luck between father and eldest daughter in the family. Should either the master bedroom or the daughter's bedroom be located in the Southeast, unexpected developments take place that lift the family fortunes higher than ever. The 6 star brings heaven's celestial blessings and good fortune for those blessed by its cosmic chi. This occurs when your bedroom is located in the Southeast; and if so, do make an effort to fill your room with yang chi energy, a higher noise level and perhaps greater movement in your room. In other words, make it vibrate with energy, as this will energize it, acting as a catalyst for good fortune to occur.

The number 6 signifies authority and power. It is associated with economics and finances. At its peak, 6 stands for authority, influence and control over money. Appearing in the Southeast, it suggests financial management does well under a mature woman.

Within the family, the year suggests that **money should be handled by women**, and power by men. On balance, the male leader has greater strength than the female, but it is the woman who holds the purse strings. This is the way the energies are laid out for the year.

Those observing this pattern of energy and flow with it are most likely to benefit from 2011. It is beneficial to bring this auspicious 6 star to life as it really benefits the entire household, especially in houses where the SE is not a tight corner or a small room that locks up its good energy.

To invoke the best kind of results from the 6 star in 2011, display the **Tree of Wealth** in the SE. Hang **6 large coins** from the tree, and if there are also **6 birds** on the tree, it signifies exciting news coming to the household.

The best way to create this effect is to find a healthy growing tree and place it in the SE before hanging auspicious symbols that ignite the intrinsic power of 6. Remember, 6 birds and 6 large coins will attract heaven luck.

Display the **Tree of Wealth** in the Southeast in 2011.

Magnifying
Victory Luck of 1 in the Northeast

The number 1 star, which brings triumph and success, flies to the Northeast corner in 2011. So anyone who resides in this part of the house benefits from this lucky star number. Anyone living here will feel its benevolent effect, as the number 1 star attracts all kinds of triumphant moments. This kind of luck is especially welcome by those engaged in competitive pursuits, as it helps you win.

In 2011 this star brings winning luck to young men, especially those who are ambitious and keen

SE	SOUTH	SW
6	2	4
5	7	9
1 VICTORY STAR	3	8
NE	NORTH	NW

to succeed. What is exciting is that the direction Northeast benefits from three good stars of the 24 mountains, so there is some very exciting potential that can be tapped from this location. It is a good idea to keep the NE energized through the year. Do not let it get too quiet. Yang energy should be created by making sure this part of the house or of your favorite room stays well lit and is occupied. At all costs, prevent *yin spirit formation* by not keeping the sector too silent through the year.

The most auspicious symbols to place here in the NE are all the symbols that signify victory such as awards, certificates, trophies and victory banners. You can also fly a flag in the NE sector this year. The flag always suggests the announcement of victories.

Place a symbol of victory like the **Victory Banner** in the NE this year. This will help you triumph over the competition and overcome any obstacles that crop up.

Benefiting from the Star of Scholarship & Romance in the Southwest

The fourth lucky secondary location of 2011 is Southwest, which benefits from the romance and scholastic star of 4. This is a very powerful star of love and will bring beautiful romantic energy to anyone residing in the Southwest. This is, in any case, the location associated with marriage and domestic happiness. It is also the place of the mother, so the matriarchal force is associated with the SW. With the romantic star 4 placed here, all the stress and strains

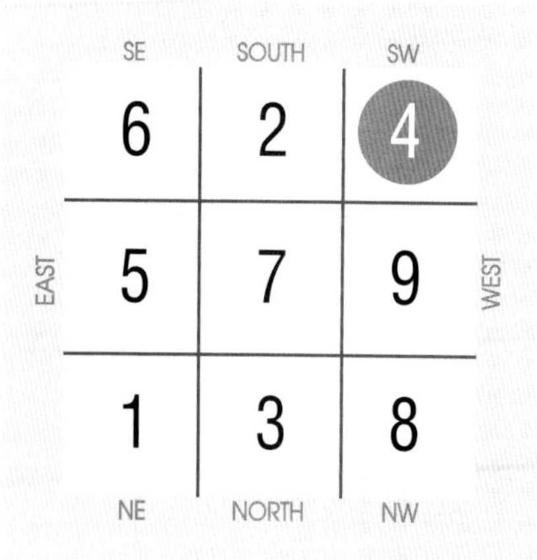
SE
SOUTH
SW
6
2
4
EAST
5
7
9
WEST
1
3
8
NE
NORTH
NW

associated with the five yellow of the past year has definitely dissolved. In 2011, this location brings love and marriage opportunities. It also brings better harmony and appreciation of the mother within families and households.

The number 4 is often associated with romantic peach blossom vibrations, so the luck of this sector directly benefits those still single and unmarried. For those already married, peach blossom brings a happier family life. Domestic energies get enhanced and those who know how to **energize the SW with bright lights** will find the number 4 star will jazz up their love relationships.

Those residing in the Northeast part of the house also benefit from the other influences brought by the number 4 star. These benefits are related to scholastic and literary pursuits, and the star brings good academic luck to those having their bedroom here. Facing Northeast is also beneficial for students and those sitting for examinations. The direction Northeast stands for wisdom and learning, so this auspicious number is a very positive star here. The only problem will be that love can also be a distraction, so if you want to enhance the scholastic side of this star, you should place literary symbols here.

Anyone involved in a writing or literary career will also benefit from being located in the NE. But do make sure you activate the sector with bright lights. Fire element energy is excellent to add to the strength of the sectors' good luck. Doing so strengthens both the romance as well as the scholastic dimensions of your fortunes in 2011. So light up this corner as best you can!

The **Chi Lin with 4 scholastic objects** is an excellent activator for the number 4 star in the SW this year, bringing education and exam luck.

Magnifying the Earth Element
to Enhance Resources

Updating feng shui each year involves more than taking care of lucky and unlucky sectors. It also requires being alert to the balance of elements and their effects on the year's energy flows. This is revealed in the year's four pillars chart which, in 2011 indicates an absence of the Earth element in the primary chart of the year.

The intrinsic element of the year as indicated by the heavenly stem of the **Day Pillar** is yang Metal, and altogether there are three Metal elements in the chart. There are also three Wood elements, one Water and one Fire, making then a total of the eight elements that make up the primary chart of the year.

The Earth element is however missing in 2011, and the Earth element symbolizes resources. This makes Earth **a very important element**, because without resources, none of the other indicated attributes such as wealth, success, prosperity, creativity and so forth can manifest.

This is one of the secrets in Paht Chee reading. It is always important that the intrinsic element (in this year, it is Metal) is kept continually replenished by having the element that produces it present.

In 2011, this means the Earth element, because Earth produces Metal; hence Earth is the resource element for 2011 (do note that this changes from year to year). As Earth is the missing element this year, anyone who makes the effort to magnify the presence of Earth element in their living spaces is bound to enjoy excellent feng shui. And Earth element is best symbolized by either a **picture of mountains** or better yet, having the presence of crystals, stones and rocks which come from within the earth.

This is the key that unlocks the manifestation of other kinds of luck. It is important to create the presence of Earth element objects in the home and to also strengthen the Earth element corners of the home. These are the Southwest and Northeast. Keep these two corners of the home well lit so that the Fire element is ever present to effectively strengthen these Earth element sectors.

The paht chee chart does however show that there is hidden Earth, but here, the Earth element is not immediately available. Nevertheless, it does indicate the availability of hidden resources. When the Earth element gets magnified, the economics of your living situation becomes extremely comfortable.

So do place stones, rocks or crystals - the best are the large circular **crystal globes** - on your coffee table in the living area and then shine a light on it so that the energy of the Earth element gets diffused through the room. Also enhance all compass Earth sectors - NE and SW as well as the center - in the same way.

Creating a "*mountain*" with rocks or pebbles in an artistic way also brings excellent feng shui potential. Indeed, it is not only the Chinese who have a tradition of creating "miniature mountains" in and around their gardens and homes. Many other Eastern traditions where feng shui is popularly practiced - such as Japan and Korea - also have their own artistic recreations of mountain scenery. This always signifies the Earth element.

Create a **mountain of pebbles** in your home
to activate the all-important resource element of Earth in 2011. The
NE and SW activated this way brings valuable
hidden resource luck to the home.

Hidden Earth

We need to look at the entire paht chee chart to
highlight the element that is in most short supply;
this involves looking at all the elements of the year's
chart including the hidden elements. In 2011, there
are three elements of hidden Earth, which bring
about a magnification of the Earth element. But in
expanding the analysis to include the hidden elements,
we need to also take note of the shortage of the Water
element. So as in the previous year, the Water element
continues to be needed.

In this respect, 2011 is better than 2010, because this
year there is one Water element available (last year
Water was completely missing). The Hour pillar has

yang Water as its heavenly stem. But Water needs to be supplemented to keep the elements in good balance.

Adding to the strength of Water strengthens the Wood element for the year and this is beneficial. This is because Wood symbolizes prosperity and financial success. Hence the placement or addition of the Water element in the Wood sectors East and Southeast creates excellent wealth feng shui.

Under the Eight Aspirations formula, the SE is also the sector that stands for prosperity via the accumulation of wealth. To activate this sector, Water required, but Water without Earth is not as effective as Water with Earth! So what is required is the placement of a **Crystal Water Feature** in the SE corner. This would be then an excellent wealth energizer for 2011. Any kind of water presence for this corner in any room that you frequently use (except your bedroom) would be excellent feng shui.

Nine Wealth Gods
to Materialize Prosperity Luck

The final feng shui tip we would like to share with
readers for the year is the placement of a ship bringing
nine wealth gods sailing into your home. This has great
relevance for the year as it suggests that the winds and
waters will bring the divine personifications of wealth
luck into the home.

Wealth Gods are a very effective for symbolic
placement in feng shui folklore, and it is for this
reason that the Chinese always invite Wealth Deities
into the home. But there are certain years when the
Wealth gods are especially effective and that is when
the *Big Auspicious* stars of the 24 mountains fly into
two opposite primary directions, which is the case in
2011.

Both the North and the South sectors of every home
have, and thus can benefit from these stars; but they
work only if they can be energized by the presence
of Wealth Deities which are believed to bring good
cosmic chi into the homes. This will activate the
North-South axis. So do place the ship in a North-
South orientation within the home.

Powerful Talismans & Amulets For 2011

If you have been following the advice given in these Fortune & Feng Shui books on annual feng shui updates, you are already familiar with the time dimension of feng shui which protects against negative luck each year.

This requires overall cleansing and re-energizing of the energy of the home to prepare for the coming of a new year, while simultaneously making placement changes to accommodate a new pattern of chi distribution. Getting rid of old items and replacing with specially made new remedial cures that are in tune with the year's chi brings pristine and fresh new luck into the home.

The Sheep goes through a mixed year in 2011. You benefit from the *Earth Seal Star* of the 24 mountains constellation, with further Big Auspicious luck brought to you from your secret friend and soulmate the Horse. These are two positive indications in your chart you should try to make the most of. However you also face *Yin House* energies which you'll need to suppress with the appropriate cures. Because you also suffer from low Spirit Essence and Life Force luck this year, you'll need protective mantras and talismans to ensure you don't fall victim to spirit harm.

This is potentially an auspicious year for you when you can make big strides in your career and personal development. As such, try to carry amulets that enhance your lucky stars, while at the same time, prevent the afflictive energies directed your way from causing harm by also wielding the correct feng shui antidotes. In this section, we recommend some of the cures you will need to ensure you make the best of the coming year of the Golden Rabbit.

Use the Enhancing Mirror to Absorb the Power of 8 from the NW

The auspicious number 8 star lies in the Northwest this year, directly opposite your home location, bringing it in direct confrontation with you. Embrace this good fortune by carrying the Enhancing Mirror, which features the **Big Auspicious** word, surrounded by the sacred syllables *Om Ah Hum*; this will attract and absorb power of 8 energy from the Northwest, allowing you to directly benefit from it. This mirror will also help you capture the chi energies of the Big Auspicious coming from the right side of your chart.

This mirror works to deflect away bad luck and the evil intentions of others, something you may have to watch out for due to your low Spirit Essence and Life Force. The more successful you are, the more reason you give others to envy you. Transform negative thoughts from others into positive ones, and turn your rivals into supporters with this sacred mirror.

Suppress Misunderstandings with the Flaming Dharma Wheel

During months when the argumentative Wood star enters your chart, you could find yourself uncharacteristically hot-tempered. Losing your cool could cost you a lot this year. Ensure you don't let this star get the better of you by displaying the Flaming Dharma Wheel in your home. This wheel is the Dhamachakra eight-spoked wheel surrounded by a circle of Fire, which symbolizes Fire and Gold energy. It has the power to reduce gossip, slander and office politics, as well as to help you in the event of any courtcase or legal entanglements you may find yourself embroiled in.

Enhance Earth Energy with the Crystal Pyramid

The Sheep enjoys the blessings of the Earth Seal this year. This indication keeps you grounded and down-to-earth in a year when you could otherwise be rather flighty and out of character. Passion and romance is high on your list of priorities this year, but without the grounding energies of the Earth Seal, this could make you impetuous, even reckless when it comes to matters of the heart. For those of you who are happily married for instance, a moment of weakness could destroy everything you've carefully built up over the years. Don't let yourself succumb to temptation and bad influence outside of your marriage and your family life by displaying the sacred pyramid in the Southwest part of your home or living room.

Display the Sacred Mantra Plaque for Protection against the Cosmic Negatives

The Four Dharmakaya Relic Plaque protects you from harm and removes all the negative vibes around you, bringing you auspicious luck instead. Because you are afflicted with low Life Force and Spirit Essence this year, you can easily fall victim to wandering spirits. And when a mischievous wandering spirit gets in your hair, it could wreak a lot of havoc in your life. This plaque with the Four Dharmakaya Relic mantra protects you from such harm. Hang near your main door.

Enhance your Home Direction with the Water Globe with Tree of Life

This crystal water globe comes with the Tree of Life and the 4 Dharmakhaya mantras at the bottom. Water is the element that appears to be in short supply from the year's Paht Chee chart, so having this water globe will help redress the balance of energies, allowing you to take full advantage of your positive luck this year. The spherical shape of the globe while ensures smooth and harmonious relationships with family, friends, colleagues and within your marriage. Display this water globe in your animal sign location of Southwest, or in the center of your living room.

Dispel Three Killings Chi with the 3 Celestial Protectors

The three celestial guardians are the best cure for the Three Killings affliction which comes from the West in 2011. Depicted with their implements, the Chi Lin carries the Lasso, the Fu Dog carries the Hook, while the Pi Yao has the Sword. Together these three guardians will dispel the negative energy coming your way from this affliction, protecting against loss of relationships, loss of good name and loss of wealth. Display them in the West part of your living room or home and also in the West of your office.

Make Best Use of Positive Affirmations to Unleash the Power of your Subconscious

Positive words and affirmations when viewed over and over are like mantras that enter your subconscious. This year we have incorporated these affirmative and positive sayings into several of our new items as powerful activators of good luck. Our glass pebbles and mandala stones with positive words and auspicious symbols can be displayed in your animal sign location of Southwest for best effect.

Put them in a pot or bowl in the SW, or even better, load them onto a miniature sailing ship, letting the ship sail in from one of your good directions. You can also add these stones into your mandala offering set.

Sacred Moving Mantra Watches

Moving mantra watches are suitable for any animal sign; anyone can wear them. These watches have been specially designed to bring you the trinity of luck - heaven, earth and mankind luck. There are 3 clocks in this watch, so it can support 3 time zones, but even better, around each dial is a mantra which moves, so every second that passes is like chanting an auspicious mantra. The mantras featured on this watch are the Amitabha Buddha mantra, Manjushri mantra and the Kuan Yin mantra. Wearing this watch will bring protection as well as attract plenty of good fortune and prosperity continuously into your life.

Also available this year are the **Medicine Buddha watch** and the **Green Tara** watch. The **Medicine Buddha watch** has been specially designed to bring good health and longevity, and it comes with the Medicine Buddha mantra and image. The band is embossed with the Medicine Buddha mantra. The mantra is repeated on the face in a moving dial so the mantra is constantly moving. Wearing this watch will bring you protection from sickness. Suitable for those of you who may be prone to falling sick, or the more elderly among you, to maintain a long, healthy and comfortable life.

The **Green Tara watch** features the beautiful Green Tara in the face. The band of the watch is stamped with Green Tara's mantra - Om Tare Tuttare Ture Soha. This mantra is repeated in a dial on the face which is constantly moving, creating blessings for you all hours of the night and day. Green Tara brings success luck and helps to overcome blocks and obstacles to success. She is also known as the Swift Liberator, known to bring results quickly to those who call on her help.

Table Top Treasures
to Enhance Desks and Workspaces

Many of us spend a great deal of our time at our desks and in front of our computers whether during work, play or our spare time. It is always good to energize the immediate space around us with good fortune symbols and items that hold positive meaning for us. We have designed two such items that make simply the most delightful table top treasures, a **miniature photo frame** enameled with peonies, the flower of love, and a **matching clock**. Place photos of your loved ones in such photo frames near you while you work. This will bring you positive and happy energy, and when you're happy, you become more productive, more peaceful and yes, also more lucky.

Powerful Gemstones
to Connect Your Lucky Day
with the Seven Most Powerful Planets

The seven planets signify seven days of the week, and connection with each planet is achieved by wearing its correct gemstone. Using your lucky day of the week, you can determine which planet has the luckiest influence on you and which gemstone you should wear or carry close to your body to attract the good luck of that planet. Start wearing the gem on your lucky day and empower with incense and mantras before wearing.

The SUN is the planet of Sunday

This is the principal planet which gives light and warmth, brings fame and recognition and enhances one's personal aura. It is an empowering planet that brings nobility, dignity and power. This gemstone enhances your leadership qualities and increases your levels of confidence so your mind is untroubled and clear. The color that activates the SUN is RED, so all red-colored gemstones are excellent for those of you having SUNDAY as your lucky day based on your Lunar Mansion.

Rubies, red garnets, rubellites or even **red glass** or **crystal** would be extremely powerful. You can also wear red clothes, carry red handbags to enhance the energy of the Sun, but a red gemstone is the most powerful… Start wearing on a Sunday at sunrise after reciting the mantra here 7 times.

Mantra: *Om Grini Suraya Namah Hum Phat*

The MOON is the planet of Monday

The moon has a powerful influence on your mind, your thoughts and attitudes. Lunar energy is associated with the tides and with water, bringing enormous good fortune to those who successfully activate its positive influences; and is especially suitable for those whose lucky day is Monday.

For energizing lunar energy, the best is to wear the pearl, those created in the deep seas or from the freshwater of rivers. Wearing pearls (any color) bring good habits to the wearer and creates good thoughts. It brings calm, peace of mind, mental stability and good health. It also brings wealth and enhances all positive thoughts. Over time, it engenders the respect of others. Start wearing on a Monday in the evening before sunset and recite the mantra here 11 times.

Mantra: *Om Som Somaya Namah Hum Phat*

The Planet MARS rules Tuesday

This is a masculine planet associated with fiery energy and the power of oratory. Activating Mars brings an authoritative air of leadership and confidence like a general leading troops to war. It brings success and victory in any competitive situation. Worn on a Tuesday, a gemstone that resonates with Mars unleashes all its fiery strength in competitive situations. The most powerful gemstone to activate Mars is **natural red coral,** the deeper the red, the better it will be. Start wearing on a Tuesday one hour after sunrise and after reciting the mantra here 19 times.

Mantra: *Om Ang Anghara Kaya Namah Hum Phat*

The Planet MERCURY rules Wednesdays

To anyone who can successfully activate Mercury, this planet brings great intelligence and amazing analytical capabilities that become vastly enhanced. Mercury increases your ability to learn and your powers of absorption are magnified. The ability to memorize also improves. Mercury facilitates powers of expression and communication. You will work fast and become effective in getting things done. The cosmic color of Mercury is green, **emeralds, green tourmalines, green quartz** are all suitable. **Green jade** is the most powerful energizer of Mercury. Anyone wearing jade will always be smarter than others and can always outwit anyone. It is a very powerful gemstone. Start wearing on a Wednesday two hours after sunrise and recite the mantra here 9 times.

Mantra: *Om Bhrum Buddhaya Namah Hum Phat*

The Planet Jupiter rules Thursdays

The most auspicious of the seven planets, this planet attracts wealth and brings great influence to those who can successfully activate its powerful energies. To do so requires you to perform many charitable works and then you will need to wear the gemstone of Jupiter that will make you rise to spectacular heights of success. You will become a highly respected leader wielding power and great influence.

Jupiter's energies are transmitted through yellow gemstones the most powerful of which are **yellow sapphires, citrines, topaz** or **flawless yellow-coloured glass** or **crystal**. Wear a yellow sapphire that is flawless and is at least 7 carats big. This brings enormous wealth luck. **Yellow Citrines** or **Imperial Topaz** are also effective. But they must be flawless or you will be quick-tempered and hard to please. Start wearing on a Thursday an hour before sunset after reciting the mantra here 19 times.

Mantra: *Om Bhrim Bhrihas Pataye Namah Hum Phat*

The Planet Venus rules Fridays

This is the planet of love, romance, sexuality, marriage, material comforts, domestic bliss and luxury. Venus brings all kinds of artistic skills to those whose lucky day is Friday and also to those who empower Venus by connecting to it via the wearing of its gemstones. Venus transmits its cosmic energy through flawless diamonds, quartz crystals, zircons, white sapphires, and other colorless gemstones with clear transparency.

Various subtle hues such as pink, yellow and blue tints are suitable for different types of professions and social positions, as long as the gem does not have any solid color. So it is crystalline stones that resonate best with Venus. Start wearing on a Friday at sunrise after you recite the mantra here 16 times.

Mantra: *Om Shum Shukraya Namah Hum Phat*

The Planet Saturn rules Saturdays

This planet governs careers and an empowered or energized Saturn is excellent for overcoming obstacles at the work place. When projects or bosses cause you to stumble or when hindrances stand in the way, it is because Saturn has to be appeased. Those whose lucky day is Friday possess the ability to rise above hardships and obstacles, but enhancing Saturn by wearing its gemstone will empower you even more. Anyone wearing Blue Sapphires can connect directly with Saturn.

Start wearing on a Saturday 2 and a half hours before sunset and recite the mantra here 23 times.

Mantra: *Om Sham Shanay Scaraya Namah Hum Phat*

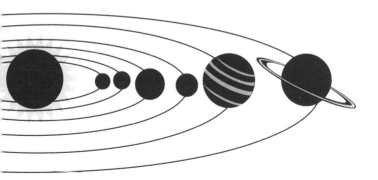

So, What Do You Think?

We hope you enjoyed this book and gained some meaningful insights about your own personal horoscope and animal sign... and you've put some of our feng shui recommendations into practice! Hopefully you are already feeling a difference and enjoying the results of the positive actions you have taken.

But Don't Stop Now!

You can receive the latest weekly news and feng shui updates from Lillian herself absolutely FREE! Learn even more of her secrets and open your mind to the deeper possibilities of feng shui today.

Lillian too's free online weekly ezine is now AVAILABLE

Here's how easy it is to subscribe:
Just go online to www.lilliantoomandalaezine.com and sign up today!

Your newsletter will be delivered automatically
to your website.

And there's more!

When you subscribe to my FREE Mandala
Weekly Ezine you will receive a special
personalized BONUS report from me... but it's
only available for those who register online at
www.lilliantoomandalaezine.com!

DON'T BE LEFT OUT! Join Today!

Thank you for investing in yourself and in this
book. Join me online every week and learn how
easy it is to make good feng shui a way of life!

This booklet tells the stories of people v

LIFE BEYOND C/

According to Department of Transport statistics, 67% of UK households have a motor car. That leaves millions of people who do not have a private vehicle parked in the driveway.

In fact, the majority of the population of Britain rely on buses and trains for getting around. In a typical car-owning household, one person drives away each morning leaving the rest of the family to walk, cycle or use public transport for their daily journeys. Many are unable to drive: the young, the infirmed, persons with visual difficulties and so on. Increasing numbers simply do not wish to drive on today's dangerous, congested roads.

None of us can escape the consequences of an unchecked growth in motor traffic; we breathe the fumes, suffer the noise and complain bitterly when our favourite stretch of countryside is threatened by a new road scheme. If we own a car, we should consider cutting out unnecessary journeys and using public transport where convenient. Anyone who drives less than around 5,000 miles a year would be better off not owning a car at all, using a hire car or taxi whenever the need dictates.

So take a train or catch a bus. Relax, leave the driving to someone else and turn the pages of this book. We'll show you the way to a **LIFE BEYOND CARS!**

Jane and David Henshaw of Castle Cary, Somerset

FAITHFUL FOUR LEGGED (AND TWO WHEELED) FRIENDS

My wife Jane and I work as 'animal sitters' for the Animal Aunts agency in Hampshire; it's a job that involves looking after a client's home and pets for anything up to three weeks. We travel almost constantly, mostly in London and in the South East, but with occasional forays into the Midlands and the West Country.

When we took up the job in 1989 we travelled almost exclusively by car (a time-expired Citroen 2CV), only taking the train when working separately. However, increasing traffic chaos and a Government forecast of a seemingly unending rise in traffic made us think again, and we reduced our car mileage from 12,000 miles a year to 6,000 over 18 months or so. By and large, we achieved this by cutting out car travel into London altogether, buying a house within walking distance of a mainline station, and taking the train for shopping trips and leisure journeys - thanks to the Network SouthEast Railcard allowing a one-third fare reduction outside peak hours in the Network SouthEast area.

1992 turned out to be an eventful year. Most of our clients were supportive, although we lost one within weeks, because they were concerned that rail-borne house sitters would be unable to take their dog to the vet in an emergency. There was, however, a car on the premises at all times!

In September we were very glad of our little car when Jane suffered a broken foot during an argument with a fractious pony. In the rush that followed, from a remote corner of East Sussex for X-rays and treatment in Eastbourne - and back the next day for a check-up we covered a total of eighty miles. But here too, we could have borrowed a car, or made other arrangements.

1

Like so many others, we had long claimed that our car was essential. But that feeling gradually evaporated, and we realised that a green transport lifestyle was perfectly possible. We reduced our reliance on the car further still, until rail mileage (and expenditure) far exceeded that on the road. However, we still needed to travel to remote locations once in a while, and that problem looked insoluble.

The real breakthrough came in October 1992 when we discovered the Brompton folding bicycle. Twenty-five pounds in weight, the Brompton could be carried on any train (and most buses) without booking or fees, and accommodate a mountain of luggage. Suddenly almost any destination in the South East was a practical proposition, and our 2CV began to take root in the garden. We needed a second folder of course, and our travel system was completed with the addition of a converted shopping trolley to the fleet, for the carriage of extra luggage.

In January 1993 we used the car for the last time - ironically for a difficult journey into central London to bring Merlin, Pippa and Chaucer (a dog and two cats of our acquaintance) down to the country for the weekend. The following day we took the plunge into a car-less existence and cashed in the tax disc on the 2CV. We didn't have the heart to scrap the car - it's still in the garden.

The disadvantages? Well, there's the cost. Even with the faithful Network card, a Young Persons card, and Boots Travel Vouchers, we found that we were slightly worse off overall. But then our car could hardly have cost less to run - most people would probably find otherwise. Some journeys take longer; road traffic makes cycling hazardous at times; timetabling can be complex; and we sometimes feel like social outcasts explaining that we do not have a car, which is sad, but inevitable.

The advantages? Travelling by bike and train brings an inexplicable sense of freedom, and the opportunity to laugh at traffic jams and parking fracas. Some journeys are quicker; a few clients are genuinely impressed; we get to chat to fellow travellers; and we usually unwind with a pint of Guinness on the way home!

TRAVEL

Memo to Managers: expecting employees to use company cars is not only costing you a great deal of money, it is subjecting them to hazards far beyond any dangers in the workplace! Some companies give travelcards or vouchers as incentives to employees to take the train or bus on business trips.

2

Clive Mowforth of Dursley, Gloucestershire gives us

DOCTOR MOWFORTH'S PRESCRIPTION

I'm 36, with professional qualifications, a good job, a wife, two young children and a large black labrador - someone who's bound to have a car, you might think. Well, you would be wrong. Despite having a driving licence, I'm proud to say that I've never owned a car.

My father was keen on railways. He bought a house overlooking Hornsea station in East Yorkshire, and commuted to Hull by train until Beeching came along. The car then became the family's sole means of transport and my father virtually lost the use of his legs.

When I was 18 I began a two year course at college in Hull, commuting each day by bus and taking the train once or twice a month to Gloucester to see my wife-to-be. I always returned late on Sundays from Gloucester and never once missed the last bus from Hull - quite a record! This was my first real introduction to railways.

The first ten years of my married life were all spent within reach of the InterCity network, first in Exeter, then in Oxford and finally in Wilmslow. This last town, being on the edge of Manchester, was well served by buses and trains - there was even a good service on Sundays during the summer giving access to all parts of the Peak District. So when I moved to Dursley (a small town in rural Gloucestershire) six years ago, my mother-in-law said 'Clive's bound to buy a car now'. I think she was surprised to be proved wrong.

Of course, your transport needs depend very much on where you live. I chose the nearest town to my place of work that was served by the company bus and that was also within easy cycling distance. Dursley also has an hourly bus service to the nearby shopping centres of Stroud and Gloucester and there's a service to take our children to school on the other side of the town - they started using the bus on their own at the age of five. Our house is just 200 yards from the bus stop, and is also close to the wooded hillside behind the town - again this was a deliberate choice.

It is amazing what shopping you can tackle without a car. For example, if I'm in Gloucester and about to return home by bus I may nip into Sainsbury's and grab 2 large packets of Persil (12 kg), or pick up 20 packets of muesli from Asda (15 kg). With a rucksack, I can easily transport over 25 kg of groceries, even though I suffer from arthritis.

The most awkward load I've transported was a 7-foot length of window board. It was too long to go on the bus, so I walked 1 1/2 miles to Gloucester station. I then caught the train to Stonehouse, and walked the eight miles to Dursley with the piece of wood perched upright in my rucksack - I received some funny looks.

We will use the train for longer trips though we do miss the advantages of living

3

close to a station. we'll usually catch a bus to the station, returning by bus or, if it's late, by taxi. If I'm on my own I may cycle the eight miles to Stonehouse - this has allowed me to spend whole days in London (8.15 am to 6.00 pm).

These journeys should become much easier in the near future with the reopening of our local station. I'm so keen on this project that I helped form a local action group last year. We've had plenty of publicity and tremendous support from local councils. We hope work will start at the site this year. The journey times to Gloucester and Bristol will be so short that most of the expected passengers will be transferring from cars.

Our main leisure activity requiring transport is rambling. You soon become adept at the necessary planning and most places in South Gloucestershire and North Avon can be reached by bus. The lack of a car has distinct advantages - you don't have to return to your starting point so you can cover large stretches of countryside. Apart from the kids, who don't like walking, our main problem is the lack of Sunday buses. We overcome this by setting aside this day of the week for jobs around the house, gardening and local walks.

Unfortunately, I can't avoid using a car altogether. I occasionally need one to visit other remote company sites, and we may sometimes hire one for family trips - at Christmas, for instance, when public transport grinds to a halt.

So we manage quite well without owning a car. Public transport may not always be very convenient, and it may take a little longer, but what does that matter? What would we do with the 10 minutes or half hour that we'd save on each trip? We are undoubtedly better off financially, but most of all we are healthier and have a clear conscience. I don't particularly want to go around polluting the atmosphere, destroying the countryside with new roads and killing off my fellow citizens. The health benefits are considerable - you do more walking so you stay fit, you avoid some of the chemical pollution, you avoid the stress of driving, and the risk of being killed or injured is much reduced.

TRAVEL

Calling car owners: we don't expect you to rush out and sell the family runabout straight away. Why not identify one journey you make regularly and see if you can get there just as easily on foot or by public transport? Phone transport operators for quotations - many travel bargains (eg 10 tickets for the price of 8) are not advertised.

TIP

TRANSPORT CAMPAIGNER ON THE MOVE

Until I was 17 I was a pretty anonymous figure at school. My only claim to fame was in tennis where I managed, just once, to take a set off a fellow pupil who went on to become the East of Scotland Junior Champion! But around my seventeenth birthday, I caused a bit of a stir ...I objected to the AA being invited to address the pupils. Loudly, and not particularly coherently (although I didn't think so at the time), I made it clear that we were getting nothing but pure propaganda, and that I was proud to be a bus user. Concerned at the antics of their wayward son, my parents promptly paid for a series of driving lessons. I had a couple...and then asked for the deposit back. I still haven't worked out if I or the instructor was the more relieved!

Almost a quarter of a century later, I'm still proud to be a bus user. In fact the thought of not being able to regularly use a bus, train, tube, bike or my two feet fills me with foreboding. To move around in a car all the time would mean I'd miss out on so much. Not that I don't gratefully accept - and even ask for - the occasional lift. In the late, dark hours of a cold winter's evening I've been known to succumb with some relish!

But, generally, the wee small hours would not be the same without London's night buses. Who would miss such a party on wheels? A bus, dramatically hurtling through the night, full of revellers singing, smooching, swaying, the sweet smell of the forbidden weed wafting down from the back seat. It beats buying petrol and a Mars Bar at a cold and deserted Filling Station anytime. And during the day, too, who would miss the hustle and bustle of life on the bus? The gossip, the arguments, the talent, the constant movement. It can be a bit slow, I grant you. But you adjust your life accordingly. And travelling becomes part of life, not simply the means of reaching your destination.

Then there is the underground life of the tube. A chance to look at the football results, complete the crossword, finish that novel, catch the eye of a particularly attractive fellow passenger. When I was still 17.....ah, but that's another story; suffice to say many a match is made on the tube. Not for me the Hollywood image of fair hair blowing in the wind as the MG sports car cruises down the freeway!

But, perhaps above all, who would exchange the sensual sights and sounds of a railway station for the bland anonymity of the M1 or the M6 ? Earlier this year I visited the Welsh Valleys. I was driven back from Merthyr to catch my train at Cardiff along a soulless motorway that cruelly cut through the heart of Pontypridd before slicing its way into the Welsh capital. I could have been virtually anywhere in the western world. On my previous visit to Merthyr, when I went by train, I could only have been in Wales.

I am still relatively young and I am able-bodied. If I were not I might appreciate a car. Right now I appreciate the real freedom I have to experience life at its fullest as I go around. Quite simply, I just don't want a car!

Faith Lawson of South London goes

WALKING FOR FUN

Nowadays nearly all my journeys begin on foot. It was not always so - for many years I did a lot of driving, but some seven or eight years ago I decided my deteriorating eyesight made me a danger to myself and others when I was at the wheel of a car, so, with some sense of relief I gave up my mini and took to walking and public transport. Because I had the foresight to get myself a home in an area which is well served by British Rail, London Underground and London Buses I do not feel in the least deprived by not having a car. I can go where I want to - and do not suffer from smelly hands after visiting a self-service petrol station, the problem of searching for a legal and convenient parking place, nor the hassle of the MoT Test, getting repairs and servicing at a reasonable price, and car crime generally! Let joy be unconfined!

Walking down the street from one's home to the station or the bus stop or the shops can be very interesting: meeting friends and acquaintances, and passing the time of day or picking up local intelligence: observing old residents leaving, and new ones arriving, and houses being split up into flats, or turned back into family houses again: seeing how the gardens grow with the changing seasons: and sometimes having a short chat with those brave people who work on the streets. They do all sorts of intriguing and useful things like bringing electricity to new lighting columns, mending cracked water mains and leaking gas pipes, and lopping trees and reducing the bits they cut off to tiny pieces in a noisy shredder - I discovered from one of these men that they spread the chippings on the Common and they eventually recycle the branches into good fertile earth. I admire all these people who work in the public gaze - sometimes an antagonistic one! - but I think the ones I admire most are the BT engineers who sort out the myriad of little coloured wires in those metal cupboards at street corners.

When I turn the other way out of my front gate I usually have my two lovely mongrel dogs with me, bound for a romp and a sniff on the Common: my local council has classified its open spaces according to whether dogs are forbidden to go there, or must be on a lead, or can run free and meet their doggy friends. Fortunately the bit of Common within five minutes walk of my house is designated "Paradise for dogs and their People". We can let them off the lead and allow them to run free with their pals and investigate all the best smells - messages left by other dogs, foxes, squirrels, birds, and odd ends of sandwiches and crisps discarded by human beings.

Their accompanying people have time to stand and chat, or sit and enjoy a rural scene in central London on part of a vast tree trunk left after the great storm of 1987, observe the bulbs and bushes and trees as they burgeon in spring and fade away again in autumn. And it is a place where you can exercise the mind quietly in a peaceful setting - a quiet walk on the Common can produce good and constructive thoughts, and we would all be a lot better off if everybody could take time out of the rat race of life to wander and ponder with only bird-song as background noise.

Walking is an enjoyable activity, even through the busy streets of a great urban sprawl: walking provides healthy exercise, needs no special equipment and no extra fuel, and pedestrians omit neither noxious fumes nor loud noises. People walking along the footway very rarely kill or maim each other in collisions - unlike the nation's favourite toy, the motor car! Moreover, occupants of cars are sealed off from the real world out there, and are not in a position to converse with each other as they journey. People are much more interesting than machines and it is time we all got back into touch with our neighbours and friends and other passers-by, by walking more and driving less - let's all walk to work, and school, and to the shops, and the bank and building society, and church.

TRAVEL

To save money, avoid premium routes and premium times of the day or week. For example, BR offer cheaper fares 'not via London' (you can go from the Midlands to the South via Reading). Travel is usually cheaper after 10 o'clock and rail Saver tickets cost more if you travel on a Friday.

Graham Nalty of Derby

DOING THE BUSINESS

Many business travellers use cars when their lifestyles would be enhanced if they went by train. Many are ensnared in the company car trap where they are provided with a car and expected to use it. Others are owner drivers who respond to the cash incentive of being paid high mileage allowance rates. Self employed people like me often use the car as a matter of habit.

When my business expanded into manufacturing audio amplifiers, I expected to visit hi-fi shops around Britain by car so I could give demonstrations. But it soon became apparent that car travel was very tiring.

On one occasion I drove from Derby to Cambridge, hitting the Nottingham rush hour and taking almost an hour to get round the city and then on to Stafford, catching the worst of the M6 evening peak on the way. By 9pm I was already in bed exhaust-

ed. The following day I had an appointment in Bournemouth and travelled by train from Birmingham International. That evening I was able to join friends in Derby at the pub, fully refreshed thanks to a relaxing train journey!

I decided to try a combination of car and train to visit customers in places like Watford and Radlett. I drove 30 miles to Nuneaton where I got the train which took one hour to get to Watford. To visit another good customer, I drove 30 miles to Loughborough, then took an InterCity train to Luton, switching to Thameslink for the trip to Radlett.

A big problem in changing from car travel to rail is carrying all the samples and paperwork needed for a day's business. When travelling by train, you can only take as much as you can carry. First you have to decide exactly what you need. Then pack it so it can be easily carried by hand. To carry audio amplifiers, I designed a simple wire frame which could hold up to three amplifiers.

The choice of railhead to start a journey is important. The road journey needs to be reasonably free of traffic so that journey time can be accurately predicted. The station car park should have plenty of spaces. If you are carrying heavy luggage, the walk from the car park to the booking office and platform must be as short as possible.

Crossing London is a serious discouragement to rail travel. The Underground is no fun at all with two heavy cases - but I have discovered how wonderful Bromley South station and Thameslink services are, allowing me to avoid Victoria Underground station in the rush hour. Thameslink is a tremendous improvement to the quality of rail journeys through London and praise is due to all in BR who have made it a success. For journeys to the west of London, I travel via Nuneaton, Coventry and Reading. Much could be done to convince the public that investment in rail is better than spending money on an even bigger M25.

For convenience, service frequencies on all short urban routes need to be half hourly or better. When making several calls during the day, a missed train on an hourly service means that a lot of valuable working time is lost waiting for the next train.

Most people think that using a car would enable me to call on more customers during the working day. But by rail, I can start out earlier and work later because it is not so tiring. On a train, I can use time profitably; I always do my quarterly VAT returns on train journeys and also read trade magazines thoroughly. In a car, stopping to eat adds to the overall journey time.

Saver and Supersaver tickets can make rail travel very competitive. As Supersaver tickets do not allow a break on the outward journey, my usual plan is to start early enough to reach the furthest call at between 10am and 11am and work back towards Derby, breaking the journey on the return. For journeys to the South Coast, I can leave Derby at 6am and be in Brighton by 9.30am or Margate by 11am at Supersaver rates.

The wide choice of rail services available to me has made a significant, positive impact on my business enabling me to visit many long-distance customers and open new accounts as a result. I certainly would not want to drive the long distances I cover by train.

TRAVEL

Our large metropolitan districts offer really cheap, unlimited travel for one day or longer. Park and ride can be cheaper than city centre parking.

Rail Travel Centres can provide bus information for towns not served by rail - and many bus travel offices can provide rail tickets and reservations.

A GUIDED TOUR THROUGH LIFE

It is hard to know how many miles of railway track I have traversed since the early days when I had to travel between Paddington and Worcester to boarding school during the last war when, of course, it was all steam; I can remember stopping twice at all the little stations and halts as the trains were too long for most of the platforms. The extra coaches were needed for carrying the large numbers of troops.

I left school in 1948 when the return fare for the 120 mile trip was about 30 shillings - and 5 shillings to carry my trunk "luggage in advance" although it sometimes arrived after me with clothes hanging out.

I then lived in the London area, studying for a while then working. Whilst I was studying, a friend and I used to go exploring around the London suburbs in the evenings on foot and would go to the nearest underground station to get back to Notting Hill. We never had any difficulties with this as the services were very reliable and we could always find someone who knew the local area to give us directions.

Between studying and getting my first job, my father and I used to make lengthy trips on railway lines in the rural areas of North Bucks, Northants and Oxfordshire. With careful studying of the timetables, one could cover large areas of countryside with suitable stopping points. I remember travelling in the cab of a diesel unit between Banbury and Buckingham - where we hit a pheasant and the driver said he would pick it up on his return journey. I went to speak to the driver of the train we were about to board from Oxford to Witney and he stood smartly to attention - he must have thought I was some B.R. official!

Whilst working and living on my own, for some 30 years, I travelled a great deal around the London area mainly by train visiting friends, going to concerts etc. and rambling in the countryside, particularly in the Chilterns where I was often able to use one line out and another on my return, having made a cross country walk.

I retired to the Isle of Wight 7 years ago and got married 2 ½ years ago, so I now have company on my bus and walking trips. We have none of the bother of finding somewhere to park or watching out for other vehicles on these narrow, winding roads. My wife, in particular, finds friendly people to talk with on the buses and in the streets while we are shopping - our way of carrying the shopping is on our backs.

Over the years, there have been some breakdowns and cancellations of buses, trains and ferries, but I have never been stranded or unable to get home at a reasonable hour. I have had no expensive bills associated with car ownership - just a 6-monthly MoT for my guide dog!

Susan Hunt of Portsmouth

ACTIVE PERSON WITH A FULL SCHEDULE TO MEET

My need to move quickly and easily around the Portsmouth area and pursue my interests is served best by the bikes I own.

I have a 'work-horse' bike which is used for journeys where I will need to carry large or awkward loads. For instance, when off to play badminton or go swimming I need to be able to carry a large sports bag with all the paraphernalia that a girl requires for these activities. But this is no problem for me for I have adapted this particular bike in my own way. I have a metal basket on the front, an old rucksack on the side 'pannier style' and another basket on the rear. To make the rear basket deep enough for large loads I take an appropriately sized cardboard box (the type used by off-licences for bottles of sherry or wine are excellent and strong too) open up the bottom and wedge it in my rear basket. Thus, the basket has now tripled its depth and becomes much more useful.

What if you are out and about and it starts to rain? No problem - go to your local pet shop and purchase a plastic, elasticated cover used for the base of birdcages in order to prevent seed falling out of the cage, and now you have a protective covering for your cardboard box and its contents. It will also provide a certain amount of security and protection from those who may be curious as to what goods you are carrying.

All my items for recycling can easily be transported to my local Recycling Centre in one go and any shopping I may need to buy is no problem. I have even been into town to purchase a Kodak Slide Projector and attachments, quite a heavy item in itself, and returned home with it in the rear basket of my 'work-horse' so you see heavy items present no problem. I guess I have always marvelled at the way the Chinese nation utilise their bicycles to carry vast loads as a matter of course.

My second bike is of the mountain type, and I use this for faster journeys when I need to carry very little. Anything that needs to be transported is done so by a ruck-sack on my back. This bike provides me with a different style of cycling, much racier because it is much lighter and there are more speeds for me to choose from. It's great fun!! And my 'devil' inside me gets a lot of satisfaction at being able to leave car drivers way behind, as they sit in a lengthy queue of traffic, watching a mere cyclist disappearing up ahead. Now, if only I could get the rest of my family to become committed cyclists, I would see that as a real achievement!!!

Douglas Smart of Edinburgh

RETIRED SOLICITOR AND TRANSPORT ACTIVIST
Tells how to enjoy the best of British countryside by public transport.

Walking in the countryside is one of the most popular pastimes among the British public. Bookshops proliferate with walking guides and many newspapers publish descriptions of walks. With a few honourable exceptions most of the walks are circular walks intended for car owners. Two guide books, *One Hundred Hill Walks around Glasgow* and *One Hundred Hill Walks around Edinburgh*, actually state that public transport is now inadequate. While it is true that rural transport has declined over the years and many fine hill walks require a car, it is nevertheless still perfectly possible to organise excellent walks by train or combined train and bus.

There are in fact many advantages from using public transport for walks. Many linear walks can be organised using public transport to get to and from either end. Cars make such walks more difficult. There are no problems with car parking especially in the tourist honeypots and a growing problem of theft from cars is avoided. After a long walk, a relaxing and sleepy train journey home is much to be preferred to a tiring journey driving home. A non-driver can also enjoy a few thirst quenching pints if there is a decent pub at the end of a walk!

Aside from the personal advantages of walking by public transport, there are obvious environmental advantages. We should all be using the car less if only to minimise pollution. Many of our major walking areas are in danger of severe damage caused by overuse of cars.

Unfortunately, since the deregulation of bus services, passengers have had to cope with constant updates to timetables (it is to be hoped that our rail services don't suffer the same fate!). Some areas are better organised than others at overcoming this problem. Derbyshire County Council publishes an excellent timetable for all public transport in the Peak District with a post card for updates and with a route map. They have a travel club with discounts on fares. The bus services, if required to supplement train services, are reasonably frequent with some routes operating on roads closed to cars. By contrast the efforts of the Lake District to promote the use of public transport are quite pathetic.

A few examples of fine walks from public transport are worth considering. Our coastline is particularly suitable for linear walks between stations. **Dunbar** to North

Berwick and **North Berwick** to Longniddry provide excellent easy walking. The **Fife Coast** is also very accessible. The **Forth and Clyde** and **Union Canals** also provide level walks with easy reach of Glasgow and Edinburgh. A section of the Roman wall can be walked between stations on the **Newcastle** to **Carlisle**, with some road walking involved. Virtually the whole of the North Yorkshire coast from **Saltburn** to **Bridlington** provides wonderful cliff walking easily accessible from trains and buses. A Railway line which perhaps provides the most abundant walking between stations is the **Hope Valley** line in the Peak District.

In the South East most of the lines radiating from London provide many excellent walking opportunities. In particular the **Thames** footpath and the **North Downs Way** can easily be walked in sections between trains.

Perhaps B.R. should do more to promote access to the countryside by rail. I suggest that they could provide a special walker's ticket. For example to walk from Dunbar to North Berwick it is necessary to buy either singles all the way or buy a return to Drem and singles Drem to Dunbar and North Berwick to Drem. It should be possible to buy a round ticket, Edinburgh to Dunbar and North Berwick to Edinburgh at a cost mid way between the two day returns on each leg.

There are many reasons why we should be reducing our car travel and promoting use of public transport. We could all make a major contribution by leaving the car at home, or at least at a convenient station, while enjoying our hills and countryside.

Photo reproduced by kind permission of "The Scotsman"

$\mathbb{TRAVEL}$

Through ticketing (eg combined bus and ferry tickets) usually saves time and money. However, on some journeys, it can be cheaper to rebook at an intermediate point (eg to take advantage of your home zone travelcard or a bargain Apex fare which only covers part of the route).

The Way Forward...

To get the most out of Life Beyond Cars, you would do well to join up with other like-minded people in one of the many groups representing public transport users or environmental interests. Below are some of the national organisations operating in Britain covering the field of transport, with addresses for membership enquiries (they will probably put you in touch with a local group in your area):

CYCLISTS' TOURING CLUB offers a wide range of services for individuals and families, and has been campaigning to improve conditions for cyclists for over 100 years. Write to: Cotterell House, 69 Meadrow, Godalming, Surrey GU7 3HS (or telephone 0486 87217).

ENVIRONMENTAL TRANSPORT ASSOCIATION campaigns for environmentally sound transport policies and provides a road rescue service like the AA and RAC, but unlike those is not a member of the British Road Federation. The service includes cycle recovery and insurance. Write to: 17 George Street, Croydon CRO lLA.

FRIENDS OF THE EARTH strongly advocate switching funds from Britain's extravagent road building programme into public transport and better facilities for cyclists and pedestrians. Write to: FREEPOST, 56-58 Alma Street, Luton, Beds LU1 2YZ (or telephone 0582 485805).

NATIONAL FEDERATION OF BUS USERS work to develop better communication between passengers and the providers of bus services. They aim to strengthen the voice of bus users and to help individuals and user groups with local problems. Write to: Membership Secretary, Silver Birches, High Molewood, Hertford SGl4 2PL.

PEDESTRIANS' ASSOCIATION exist to encourage walking. They help local residents solve problems of getting around safely on foot and encourage local councils to provide a better environment for pedestrians. Write to: Membership Department, The Pedestrians' Association, 27 Penrith Gardens, Westbury-on-Trym, Bristol BSlO 5LX.

RAILWAY DEVELOPMENT SOCIETY campaigns for better rail services for both passengers and freight, and for greater investment in our rail network. The membership is around 3,000, with many more affiliated through rail user groups. Write to: Membership Secretary, 13 Arnhill Road, Gretton, Corby, Northants NN17 3DN.

SUSTRANS is an organisation dedicated to building new traffic-free routes linking town and city with countryside (using disused rail lines, canal towpaths, forest trails and the like); over 250 miles is now in use by walkers and cyclists. Write to: 35 King Street, Bristol BS1 4DZ (or telephone 0272 268893).

THE RAMBLERS' ASSOCIATION founded in 1935 promotes rambling, protects rights of way, campaigns for access to open country and defends the beauty of the countryside. Write to: 1/5 Wandsworth Road, London SW8 2XX.

TRANSPORT 2000 is a network of environmental groups, consumer bodies and trade unions working for integrated and environmentally-sensitive transport. They organise conferences, publish reports, lobby MPs and send out regular briefing documents. Write to: Walkden House, 10 Melton Street, London NW1 2EJ (or telephone 071 388 8386).

WHAT IS THE RAILWAY DEVELOPMENT SOCIETY?

The RDS is the only national pro-rail pressure group independent of both British Rail management and trade unions. It was formed in 1978 by the amalgamation of two long established voluntary associations, and today acts both as a campaign for a fairer share of transport investment for the railways, and as a consumer organisation representing rail users nationwide. It is not linked with any political party, and has members of all shades of political opinion.

We seek a better rail system for Britain because we believe that railways offer a safer and more fuel-efficient alternative to the uncontrolled growth of road transport for both passengers and freight; they are also much less damaging to the environment of towns and countryside, and to the health and safety of our citizens. We also believe that rail users need a voice to speak up for their interests, both with BR management and with local and national politicians who take far reaching decisions affecting their daily lives.

As campaigners we have pressed, with some success, for further electrification of the rail network; for better local and regional trains; and for the reopening of lines and stations closed to passengers. We have strongly opposed rail cuts and closures, and continue to do so, and have been at the forefront of opposition to the damaging aspects of rail privatisation. We have also done much detailed work in helping to promote the transfer of freight traffic from road to rail. The Channel Tunnel, a vital link with the rest of Europe, is a project which we strongly support.

As a consumer organisation, we have made many specific representations to BR, at local and national levels, in order to prevent deteriorations in services and to secure improvements wherever possible. We also act as a national advisory and co-ordinating body for the many local rail users' groups, holding a conference of such groups every year. We also maintain links with other bodies campaigning for better public transport, such as Transport 2000, the National Council on Inland Transport, and Friends of the Earth.

Our quarterly journal, Railwatch, is read by many interested parties outside as well as inside the RDS, as are our local branch newsletters. We publish books, reports and leaflets on particular issues, as well as a series of regional guidebooks for rail passengers which have become widely popular with the travelling public.

As a voluntary body financed almost entirely from members' individual subscriptions, we cannot match the power of the roads lobby. Nevertheless, we have made sure that the case for railways is heard, and we are determined to continue pressing for a better future for rail transport in this country.

SUBSCRIPTIONS

Standard Rate: £10; Juniors, Senior Citizens, Unemployed: £5. Special family and corporate rates are available on request. Write to the Membership Secretary at: 13 Arnhill Road, Gretton, Corby, Northamptonshire NN17 3DN.